SHOUTS FROM THE REPUBLIC

Shouts from the Republic

A Brief History of the Republic of Texas and the Cost of Freedom

BLAKE A. PFEFFER

Whitecaps Media
Houston

Whitecaps Media
Houston, Texas
www.whitecapsmedia.com

Some of the material has been derived from works now in the public domain. See Sources and Acknowledgments for further information.

The Illustration Credits page represents a continuation of this copyright page.

ISBN: 978-1-942732-30-3

Printed in the United States of America

www.texashistorybook.com

Dedicated to my great aunt Noel who lived to be 106 years old and never retired from her mission to bring Truth and Love to the world

Special thanks to friends and family who supported this effort with proofreading, fact checking, critical comment, and constructive criticism—

Chris Beavers
Felicia Boyd
Andrew Ellis
Mike Mattina
Ben Pfeffer
Jeanne Pfeffer
Kirk Pfeffer
Suzanne Pfeffer
Kit Sublett
Frank Vandiver
Ken Wise
Mike Wyatt

And especially to Jeanne, my favorite Texan, who loves me and put up with a lot while I typed

CONTENTS

It would be good for you to look back, look
to the place from where you came, the rock
out of which you were shaped and the quarry
from where you were mined.

—ISAIAH 55:1, THE VOICE TRANSLATION—

INTRODUCTION

THE HISTORY OF THE REPUBLIC OF TEXAS IS FASCINATING, and I present it here in short summary both to honor those who tamed this wilderness and to remind us that many of them gave themselves to something they valued more than their own lives—Freedom—so that future generations could live free.

From a very early age, my father instilled in me the love of Texas history. The stories read better than fiction, and I carry those memories into the present. My family can trace its Texas lineage back to Noah Smithwick—a nineteen-year-old boy who came alone to Texas from Kentucky in 1827, a blacksmith by trade, and later a Texas Ranger—whose writings you will find quoted herein, in addition to others in our lineage from Texas' past. We have farmed in Waller County since the 1940s, and we still own a small piece of an original "Old Three Hundred" Mexican land grant from Stephen F. Austin's first colony.

Our Texas roots run deep, and I cherish the gift of Freedom given to me by my ancestors, both from Texas and from the United States. In the present, I find myself wrestling with the world as I see these freedoms being challenged. That realization galvanized my need to write this history as a gift to you, just as its telling was a gift to me.

Every day I carry in my pocket a half-dollar coin minted in 1836—the year of the Texas Revolution—as a reminder to me of the price of Freedom. Etched on the face is the image of a woman wearing a cap upon which is inscribed, "Liberty." On the back is, "*E Pluribus Unum*," which translates to "Out of Many, One." It is a constant reminder to me that we are a diverse and varied people. Even more importantly, we are a people who together share in the luxury and benefits that the institution of Freedom grants to those who live under its umbrella.

Texas' rich history is full of lessons that fewer and fewer people in the present era are aware of, and therefore cannot value or appreciate. In this book I will challenge you to consider that this societal norm we call Freedom is not a universal constant which is assured to any people or nation. I will call you to recognize the high value the people of the Texas Revolutionary era placed on Freedom, both in the risks they took with their livelihoods and with their lives. As you read their stories, I ask you to consider what value you place on maintaining Freedom in the present world. Let us listen to the past and return to a common mind that will preserve Freedom for future generations. If we do not both understand and value the institution of Freedom, future generations will once again live in tyranny.

History teaches us that Freedom is not self-sustaining. It is a precious jewel that must be protected lest it be destroyed by those who wish to consolidate power. The landscape of history is littered with wreckage resulting from tyranny that follows the consolidation of political power. In context I define Freedom as the right granted to you by government, to live as you choose so long as you live within a set of societal laws that define acceptable standards of community living. In other words you can live free so long as you don't murder or steal, etc. I might add that Freedom is the right to live as you *ought* to live in deference to the rights of others. You will find "Freedom" capitalized throughout as I make reference to this ideal which has a life and value of its own, a presence that is worthy of honor, attention, and nurturing.

The Texas Revolution was a war of ideals, not a war based on race or ethnicity. Anglos and Mexicans who valued the freedoms guaranteed to them in the Mexican Constitution of 1824 battled authoritarians who were eroding their rights. Over a very few years those rights and freedoms began to be confiscated, and their fears were fully realized when the Constitution was ultimately annulled. This is the story of the path followed by these settlers, adventurers, and freedom-lovers in their journey to subdue a wilderness, establish order upon it, and ultimately reclaim the freedoms that were taken from them. They shout to us from the Republic! Hear their story.

In the narrative I make liberal use of the word "republican," spelled with a lower case *r*. Simply put, this describes anyone who favorably views a republic form of government which by definition derives its authority from the governed. Such people recognize that republics do the greatest good for the most people. The United States, for example, is a representative republic, not a democracy, although the two are very closely related. A person who views socialism, communism, or a dictatorial form of government favorably is not republican in their views. When used in the lower case, it does not directly imply association with the Republican Party of modern-day politics, nor does it imply opposition to the modern-day Democratic Party.

The ideal of republicanism commits itself to a constitutional form of government which derives its authority from the governed, guarantees Freedom to its citizens, and ensures the continuance of its jurisdiction for future generations. Settlers in Texas were almost universally republican in their views of government, and they came here under the promise of guaranteed civil rights and freedoms found in the Mexican Constitution of 1824. That, in no small way, motivated their actions before, during, and after the Revolution.

Set against the totality of world history, republican societies occupy only a tiny piece of human experience compared to the myriad ruled by tyranny. Republican societies, however, contribute exponentially more than their share to the uplifting of humanity.

The word *Texas* derives from the Caddo Indian word *tejas*, meaning "friends" or "friendly," and was also used as a greeting: "Hello, friend." As the Aztec influence in the region grew, the *j* was replaced with an *x*. It appears that the term was first applied to this geographic area in the 1600s when we find Spanish references to "a great kingdom of *Texas*." The state motto, "Friendship," traces its origins back to the Caddo.

In writing this book I have used original editions from my personal library as source material. My late father, Adolph "Bubba" Pfeffer, Jr., began collecting books on

Texas history in the 1970s, and that collection forms the core of my library. I have continued to expand and improve it, and I take great pleasure in reading from these original publications.

My desire is to deliver to you an accurate and readable overview of the Republic of Texas' history. Much of the narrative is quoted and/or compiled directly from the works of respected historians from yesteryear. My source materials are largely books published between 1833 and 1928. Due to the lapse of time and applicable copyright laws, any copyright in these materials no longer exists, and therefore, each of the works are in the public domain for others to review, copy, and quote from as freely as any new author may wish. In view of the public domain status of these books, I have quoted liberally from them. Where I have done so, I do not claim those contributions as my own but rather breathe new life into their words. Each of those sources is listed in the back, and I give credit to the original authors as it is due. My intent is to get as close to the original characters and firsthand accounts as the historical record will allow.

I ask that this brief history lesson be a reminder to you of the price of Freedom.

—Blake Pfeffer
HOUSTON, TEXAS

Mankind is ruled by oppression
Until some are willing to die
That others may live Free

I. PRELUDE TO A NATION

The discovery of the Americas in 1492 by Christopher Columbus began one of the most striking eras in world history. European nations raced for possessions in the New World for three hundred years, each basing its claims upon explorations and further discoveries. Spanish adventurers first reached the American mainland through the Gulf of Mexico. In 1682 the French explorer René-Robert Cavelier, sieur de La Salle, stood at the mouth of the Mississippi River, verbally claiming the country far and wide for his monarch. It has been said that his claim included Florida, reached across the Rockies to the northwest, and also included Texas. The latter claim is reinforced by the fact that La Salle returned to Texas in 1685 and founded a colony at Matagorda Bay, where he later died.

Following LaSalle's death and the failure of his colony, the Spanish made feeble and futile efforts at settling Texas, claiming it as part of New Spain. For the better part of the next one hundred years, Spain, England, and France staked their claims in the New World, while the port of New Orleans rose in importance as the gateway to the Mississippi River.

In the middle of the 1700s, France and England fought the French and Indian War over control of the Ohio Valley region. When it became apparent to France that

England would win, France hurriedly handed Louisiana over to Spain in 1762 to keep it from falling into the hands of England, their archnemesis. At the time Louisiana was a vast unexplored territory reaching far beyond the boundaries of the present-day state of Louisiana. Spanish sovereignty now extended to all lands around the Gulf of Mexico, including the Florida territory, Louisiana, Texas, the current nation of Mexico, and it reached far north and west towards Canada and the Pacific Ocean. Taking all of Spain's claims in the Americas, New Spain was greater in area than any nation in the world with the exception of Russia and possibly China.

At the time, the United States was not interested in expanding its footprint to the west, but it had already claimed land west to the Mississippi River and south of a horizontal line through the state of Mississippi. The right to navigate through the Spanish Territory at the mouth of the Mississippi and on to the Atlantic was of great importance to the United States, and in 1795 a treaty was concluded between the U.S. and Spain to protect that right.

Thus, as the year 1800 rolled around, England controlled Canada, and the United States was rooted along the eastern seaboard. Spain was the nominal master of the greater part of North America, which was mostly uninhabited and largely unexplored. Texas was little more than a name on a map.

Enter Napoleon, who in 1800 was thirty years old and had just conquered Italy and Egypt. Napoleon began what would become a chief occupation of his—namely "King Making." He engaged a petty young Duke from

Spain who wanted to be a king. This Duke of Parma, who had applied to Napoleon for a kingdom, was both nephew and son-in-law of the Bourbon King of Spain. And it suited the French leader's purposes to indulge him. Thus Napoleon created a kingdom out of the Tuscany region of Italy, named it Etruria, warranted it to contain no fewer than one million souls, and set up this young Duke and his wife as king and queen. Of course Napoleon extracted a fee for his services from the land-poor Bourbon King, and Louisiana was ceded back to France as compensation for the kingdom (Louisiana being very broadly defined to include, more or less, ten future American states and Texas). The deal was memorialized in a secret agreement in October 1800.

News—especially secret news—traveled slowly in that day, and it took about eighteen months for U.S. president Thomas Jefferson to confirm the rumors. He was troubled by the prospect of war-inclined France controlling the mouth of the Mississippi River through which three-eighths of the produce of the United States traveled. So the U.S. opened negotiations with France to buy a site at the mouth of the river to protect her right to use the lower Mississippi, but this effort was ignored by France. So important was this to the United States that threats were made to take it by force if necessary. Future president James Monroe was appointed envoy to France and Spain to try to buy New Orleans plus the Spanish territory east of the Mississippi River. Little mention was made of land west of the river because no one was interested in it. Negotiations went nowhere until Napoleon learned that England was planning an expedition to occupy New Orleans. France, once again, could not contemplate the thought that their New World holdings might fall into their archnemesis' hands, and Napoleon, being busy conquering the Old World, quickly sold Louisiana to the United States. We know this as the Louisiana Purchase of 1803.

Monroe was only authorized to buy New Orleans and lands east of the Mississippi River in those negotiations, but Napoleon insisted on selling the whole territory. And so it was that the U.S. representative overstepped his authority and agreed to buy five hundred million acres more than he had authority to buy, albeit at the same price that he was authorized to pay for the lesser acreage.

As strange as it is to us in the modern world, no one could say precisely what land was included in the Louisiana Purchase of 1803, or when France ceded Louisiana to Spain in 1762, or when Spain re-ceded it back to France in 1800. Boundaries were not easily defined in vast frontier claims. Inquiries were made to both France and Spain to define the exact boundaries. The answers came along the lines of "did not know," and "we must take it as they had received it." In other words, they did not know either.

Finally in 1819 by way of the Adams-Onis Treaty, the U.S. bartered with Spain to receive clear title to the Florida territory and gave up any claim it may have had to Texas by way of the Louisiana Purchase, which certainly should have been part of that deal by way of La

Salle's explorations. If the U.S. Government had openly claimed Texas as part of the Louisiana Purchase, it could have made good on the claim either by rightful title or by military strength, but the government had remained silent.

Thus in 1819, clear title and uncontested Spanish sovereignty over Texas was publicly established, setting up what would be the epic story of the Texas Revolution. News of Texas being ceded to Spain was not well received in these parts, given the local sentiment was that Texas was part of Louisiana and should remain so—Louisiana having already been admitted to the Union as a state seven years prior. Winds of revolution were stoked both from United States citizens living in the border regions and from Mexican revolutionaries who were engaged in their own struggle against Spanish oppression.

II. POLITICS, PROMISES, AND THE PURSUIT OF FREEDOM

A Filibustering Expedition

The years between the Louisiana Purchase of 1803 and the Adams-Onis Treaty of 1819 were ripe with activity and change. Uncertainty and speculation regarding the sovereignty of Texas fueled the fire but also prevented any real and permanent progress. In 1810 forces from Mexico began their long struggle for independence from Spanish persecution and this sentiment spilled over to American adventurers with visions of empire, particularly in the Louisiana border region.

Mexican revolutionaries of this era were republican in their views of government and spoke of creating a federal system like that in the United States. The idea intrigued an American lieutenant named Augustus Magee, who along with Colonel Bernardo Gutiérrez, conceived a plan to conquer Texas from Nacogdoches to the Rio Grande River to build a republic.

In 1811 an unauthorized military expedition crossed the Sabine River from Natchitoches, Louisiana, into Spanish Texas to support Mexico's republican revolution against Spain. This filibustering expedition, as these revolutionary assists were called, was not an uncommon phenomenon in the nineteenth century. Lieutenant

Magee recruited 130 men for his expedition who were mostly outlaws, vagabonds, and buccaneers from Jean Lafitte's flourishing pirate enterprise. This so-called "Republican Army of the North" achieved early military success, grew in numbers, and moved deeper into Texas in what would become the first Texas Revolution of 1811–13. A declaration of independence was signed, and an ad hoc government was formed; however, the Mexican revolutionaries did not invite the Americans to provide input into the process of forming a republican government. It resulted in a junta that was anything but democratic or republican in its nature, concentrating power in a small group of people.

In 1813 after many military successes, the Magee-Gutiérrez Expedition as it became known, culminated in the Battle of Medina—the final battle of the "First Texas Revolution." It was fought on August 18 at El Encinal de Medina, an oak grove southwest of San Antonio de Béxar about ten miles from the Medina River. (San Antonio de Béxar—pronounced bay-HAR—is the original name of the settlement at present day San Antonio, Texas, and the two terms can be used interchangeably.) The revolutionaries were soundly defeated. Out of the 850 Anglos who entered the battle, ninety percent of them were killed, only a few having escaped.

More Texan lives were lost in the Battle of Medina than in all the battles and skirmishes in the better known "Second Texas Revolution" of 1835–36, which is commonly referred to as "The Texas Revolution." Interestingly, during this first revolution, a young sub-lieutenant in the Spanish army by the name of Antonio López de Santa Anna was cited for bravery. However, the sub-lieutenant not so bravely participated in the slaughter of all republican prisoners of war after the battle was over. Santa Anna, of course, would go on to declare himself dictator of Mexico and become Public Enemy Number One of the freedoms that the colonists so passionately valued. In looking back over Santa Anna's actions in and after this battle, we can see both his rise as a military figure and also his contempt for life in the killing of all the prisoners who had surrendered. The extermination operation following the battle lasted for weeks as the Spanish forces hunted down and killed those who had fled in defeat.

The Empresario Rises

Throughout this period, roving bands of native Indians in the Texas territory were wreaking havoc on settlers and making raids deep into Mexico, as far south as Mexico City. Many of the indigenous inhabitants of this area were peace-loving and interacted with the settlers productively. Others like the Comanche, however, were warlike by nature, and the settlers simply provided a fresh target for their trade. Even the name *Comanche* gives insight into their nature. It is an Americanization of the term used by the Ute Indians to refer to that tribe, which translates along the lines of, "anyone who wants to fight me all the time." And while they were not the only Indian purveyors of bad behavior, they were certainly inclined towards violence and were the most formidable of all the tribes, not to mention that they were the best horsemen North America has ever known.

The Spanish Government and later the Mexican Government, with their large slow-moving armies and heavy artillery, were helpless to stop the fast, aggressive, and stealthy Indians. Given that Texas was a distant outpost on the frontier, neither the Spanish nor the Mexican authorities were concerned about the raids occurring in Texas, but they were greatly concerned with the raids reaching the seat of government in Mexico City. This problem would soon become a central factor in the plan to colonize Texas.

At the time the Adams-Onis Treaty was concluded in 1819, a Connecticut Yankee by the name of Moses Austin was living in Spanish Missouri as a Spanish subject. He heard that clear title to Texas had been established and conceived the idea of an American colony there. Austin traveled to San Antonio de Béxar to personally present himself to the Spanish governor for the necessary permission, arriving in December 1820. He was enamored with Texas and the prospects of starting a colony in a new world. His request, however, was quickly denied, and he was ordered to immediately leave the country.

As Austin was preparing to depart, he had a chance meeting on the main plaza with Philip Hendrik Nering Bogel, a Dutch businessman who went by the self-bestowed title of Baron de Bastrop. The Baron was in the service of the Spanish Government and had the ear of its officials. The two had met years before in a New Orleans restaurant and were happy to reacquaint. The

Baron interceded with the governor and convinced him that Austin was a faithful Spanish subject who was worthy of his request. His sway prevailed, and for the first, last, and only time, a land grant request of this kind was granted *by Spain* in the New World. Moses Austin received word that his petition to move three hundred families to Texas—"the Old Three Hundred"—had been granted while on his deathbed en route back to Missouri. He bequeathed the legacy to fulfill this commission to his son, Stephen Fuller Austin, who soon traveled to San Antonio de Béxar to accept his father's commission.

On August 12, 1821, while on his way there, Stephen Austin reached the Guadalupe River where he received word that Mexico had won its independence from Spain. During his nine-day stay in San Antonio de Béxar, he was given formal permission to continue the colonization, now under Mexican authority, in a letter dated August 12; but this written authority now came from the governor of the Mexican state. The agreement gave Austin wide authority to choose the land he wanted to colonize, both as to location and size, and to create the terms under which he would make land grants to colonists. And so it came to pass that the first and greatest empresario arose. He would spend thirteen of the next fourteen years as a faithful and loyal subject of Mexico, receiving a total of four land grants. (*Empresario* means "contractor" in Spanish and it applies here to those granted permission to give land away on authority of the government. The empresario was authorized to distribute land to settlers for the purpose of colonizing an area. He did not take title to the land, however, and acted more like a broker who screened potential settlers on behalf of the government.)

Upon Austin's return to San Antonio de Béxar in March 1822, the Mexican governor suggested that he seek the approval of the new national government in Mexico City under the leadership of Agustín de Iturbide. Austin took the advice, but he knew his journey would be perilous and difficult. He crossed the Rio Grande at Monterey on foot with one companion. Knowing the dangers of the journey, they disguised themselves as beggars with an improvised story that they were patriots who had fought in the Revolution and were traveling to seek renumeration. At the time, Austin spoke little Spanish and had only a Spanish grammar book he was using to learn the language. He had to trade it to a band of Comanche Indians along the way in exchange for safe passage. They traveled twelve hundred miles in thirty-six days. He was twenty-eight years old.

Austin had to start over with the new Mexican Government. He lobbied the First Congress for six months advising and helping to draft a colonization agreement which was within a few paragraphs of completion and days from certain ratification when, in late October 1822, Iturbide dissolved Congress, giving its members ten minutes to vacate the building. Iturbide declared himself to be Emperor and his power to be absolute, assisted only by his hand-picked junta.

Austin once again started all over. He hurriedly presented himself to the new government and by persistence and providence in January of 1823, almost two years from the date his father had received his grant, Austin's request was sent to the Emperor with a favorable recommendation.

It seemed at last that Austin would get his authority memorialized, but before he could leave the city, Iturbide's government fell, and the Emperor was marched out of the city, never to return.

Still, Austin persisted, waiting for the next government to assemble, and quickly presented himself along with his petition, uncertain of the status of his agreement from the now deposed government. He found favor with some old faces from the last Congress, and on April 14, 1823, full and final approval was given to him by the national government, being the first, last, and only *Mexican national* land grant in Texas; thereafter, land grant legislation in Texas was remanded to the Mexican state for enactment.

The revolving door of Mexican politics delayed Austin's plans nearly two years, but he now had his authority and would spend the remaining years of his life working for the people of Mexican Texas to establish and safeguard order and freedom so that its citizens could thrive. He would live less than fourteen more years, and in all but the last year of his life, he would be a faithful Mexican subject who worked to exhaustion at the expense of his own health in pursuit of these goals.

III. WINDS OF REVOLUTION

Mexican governments of this era came and went quickly and were defined by corruption, ego, and bloody power struggles. In this revolving door of leadership changes, settling and managing the Texas frontier was an issue that was hard to address cohesively. Much thought was given in Mexico City as to the wisdom of granting land to foreigners, even though they pledged allegiance to the Mexican nation. Some thought it unwise and that no people of Anglo-Saxon descent could ever culturally or religiously integrate into Mexican society. At the same time, others saw wisdom in moving Anglos into the no-man's land of Texas as a buffer between Mexico proper and the roving warlike Indians who were regularly raiding Mexico City and settlements in between. Eventually the latter position prevailed and the scheme to safeguard the Mexican interior by populating Texas with American immigrants prevailed. The sentiment was to let the Indians occupy themselves raiding the sparsely populated settlers in Texas which, the theory went, would leave Mexico proper free from raids.

And it worked! At least for a time . . .

Following the multiple dictatorial disasters of early Mexican governments, Mexico moved to a republican form of government by adopting the Constitution of 1824. Among other things, and in order to facilitate immigration to Texas, civil rights and freedoms were constitutionally guaranteed to immigrants who would settle in Texas.

These rights largely mirrored the U.S. Bill of Rights, granting the freedom to bear arms, freedom of assembly, freedom of speech, etc., but notably did not initially include freedom of religion. Catholicism was the national religion of Mexico, to which one had to pledge allegiance; all other religions were prohibited. These rights and the promise of free or very cheap land incentivized Americans to immigrate to Texas. They came by the thousands, and the plan worked well initially, although Mexico's anxiety about the possibility of a settler revolt increased proportionally to the increase in the Anglo population in Texas, which would eventually grow to be six times the number of Mexicans living there. As the calendar turned towards the end of the 1820s, Mexican concerns culminated in the Decree of 1830, also known as the Law of April 6, which forbade all future immigration to Texas by Americans.

The decree was largely ignored between 1830 and 1832, as Americans continued to come freely to Texas, but those that came were not allowed citizenship nor were they eligible to receive land grants (Stephen Austin's colony was excepted from the decree). The decree caused much discontent among the Anglo population.

The Settlers' Society

The life of a settler who moved to Texas was one of difficulty, and by its very nature, that life was focused on survival. The early immigrants were, almost without exception, poor and had to work with their own hands to provide the basic necessities of life. They had moved to Texas in hopes of bettering their condition and even owning land, and they were willing to go to great lengths in pursuit of that dream. In the meantime there were no banks, no hotels, no grocery stores, and no homes to occupy. There was no law other than some general codes drawn up by Stephen Austin, no standing police force, and no court system.

The settlers often administered their own justice, or at best handed criminals to the town *alcalde*—the chief civil officer who presided over the *ayuntamiento*, the local town council (however, the first *ayuntamiento* was not established until 1828 in San Felipe, at which time the first election ever held in Texas occurred). There were no fences, given that barbed wire was not even patented until 1867, and no communication but by word of mouth. There were few towns in the early days and few establishments from which to buy goods. There was only you, land, and natural resources you could use to build shelter and to tame and improve the land. For upwards of a year, no one in Austin's colony even possessed a plow. Corn was planted with a stick.

In 1823 Stephen Austin announced that he would pay out of his own pocket for "ten men . . . to act as rangers for the common defense . . . [at] fifteen dollars a month payable in property." He took this action because Mexican efforts to secure the frontier colonies were wholly inadequate and ineffective. These rangers were required to provide their own weapons, horses, saddles, and personal effects. They assembled when significant atrocities against the citizens presented themselves and then disbanded until the next situation demanded their attention. When called into action, the largely unregulated force often acted unilaterally as judge, jury, and executioner. Rangers hailed from Anglo, Hispanic, and Indian roots, and each heritage was known to hold all ranks within the ranger companies.

In the settlers' world of frontier life where theft of a horse or other basic necessity could mean the difference between life and death, rangers brought brutal order into the chaos of crimes against Texas humanity. They came to be known as *Los Diablos Tejanos*—"the Texas Devils." While citizens were largely responsible for policing their own worlds, the rangers provided an efficient and effective neutralizing force against greater threats to the emerging society. Austin's rangers were the precursor to the current Texas Rangers which were officially sanctioned by the Provisional Government of Texas in October 1835.

Well-intended people who sought a life in this frontier environment were by nature independent, adaptable, self-sustaining, and generally possessed a moral code that brought order to the unregulated environment. By necessity, settlers had to be farmers, hunters, and gatherers to merely survive, and life was a constant effort to sustain themselves individually and communally given the many deprivations afforded by this existence. In these settlers' societies, those with hospitality and neighborly kindness were highly regarded, while loners were pushed to the bottom of the social scale.

Early settlers describe immense herds of buffalo and wild horses, but these were often not useful to them due to the hardship, risk, and expense of attempting to capture or kill them, and because it could be seen as an affront to the already hostile Indians. In his writings to advise others who might consider coming to Texas, a lawyer named A. A. Parker wrote that the immigrant should "carry with him bread stuffs to last six months," but that "cattle and hogs are plenty and wild game abundant." The currency that was preferred by the immigrants was U.S. gold and silver coins.

The majority of those who immigrated to Texas sought to acquire land upon which to establish themselves, a quiet life of agriculture, and/or the adventure of taming a new country in which they could live under similar constitutional freedoms they had enjoyed in the United States. Other less noble immigrants sought to escape unpaid debts or even flee legal prosecution, but those elements did not define the population. By and large their politics were simple: Give us freedom and representation and leave us alone to pursue life as good Mexican citizens.

Mary Austin Holley, a cousin to Stephen, in a letter dated December 1831, wrote the following about the political state of Texas:

> ... it is not at all difficult to determine what, in all likelihood, will be the future destiny of Texas. Should

> the Mexican government adopt a correct policy in relation to this country [meaning if the government affirmed the constitutional guarantees in the Mexican Constitution of 1824], it [Texas] will form a valuable and efficient state of the Mexican federation, for under a judicious system of administration, it would not be in the interest of the inhabitants to dissolve the present connection, and they could feel no motive to do so.

The simple translation: If the Mexican Government's politics and policies towards Texas are left as they were originally represented, both the government and the citizens will be content.

> It is very possible, however, that an unwise course of administration on the part of the general government ... might provoke a separation ... If unmolested in their lawful pursuits of industry, and protected by equal laws from the imposition of the federal officers, they will be satisfied ...

The simple translation: If the government reneges on the people's constitutionally-guaranteed civil rights, they will rebel; but if left alone and treated fairly, they will be satisfied as Mexican citizens.

Holley's views largely represented the feelings of settlers who had come to Texas to plant their roots on the land and establish themselves long-term. It can be said, however, that those who came for adventure were more inclined to favor an immediate fight for independence.

In another letter dated that same month, Holley, in speaking of Moses and Stephen Austin's moving Anglo-Americans into the Texas territory, says,

> ... and whatever good may result to the great cause of liberty, of science, and human happiness, by the introduction into this vast region, of the English language, and of those principles of republican and constitutional government, which always accompany that language, may be very properly attributed to them [the settlers].
>
> The settlers of Austin's colony were unaided by capital or support, either from the Mexican government or from any other quarter. They had no resources, whatever, to depend upon, except those afforded by the spirit and prudence of their leader [Stephen Austin], a total contempt of danger, obstacles, and privations, and a firm reliance upon their rifles, themselves, and their God. Besides the natural difficulties of subduing the wilderness, they had to contend with deeply fixed prejudices [that the Mexicans held against the Anglos, and] ... the revolutionary and distracted condition of the civil government in Mexico.
>
> Until recently, neither the Mexican government nor the Mexican people knew anything of this interesting country, and, whatever value it now possesses in their estimation, or in the opinion of the world, is to be attributed, entirely, to the foreign emigrants. They redeemed it from the wilderness—they developed its resources—they have explored it, in its length and

> breadth, and made known its geography. All has been done by them, without the cost of a single cent to the Mexicans.

These sentiments were confirmed by Mexican Colonel Juan Almonte, who was commissioned to make a general inspection of Texas in 1834. His conclusions were published in 1835 and include the following:

> If we consider the extraordinary and rapid advances that industry has made ... the conclusion is that Texas must soon be the most flourishing section of the [Mexican] Republic. There is no difficulty in explaining the reason of this prosperity. In Texas, with the exception of some disturbers, they only think of growing [various crops listed], the breeding of cattle, opening of roads, and rendering the rivers navigable. Moreover, the effects of our political commotions are not felt there ... The inhabitants of that country continue, without interruption, to devote themselves to industrious occupations, giving value to the lands with which they have been favored by the munificence of the government.

He goes on to say,

> Money is very scarce in Texas; not one in ten sales is made for cash. Purchases are made on credit, or by barter ... Trade is daily increasing, owing to the large crops of cotton, and the internal consumption, caused

by the constant influx of emigrants from the United States.

Both accounts put sharp focus on how industrious and orderly the Anglo population was. And these traits were essential to survival in an untamed frontier wilderness in which there was little civil authority. Almonte noted the 1834 population of San Antonio de Béxar to be twenty-four hundred, and the population of Goliad, seven hundred.

A Political Petition Takes Shape

In 1832 Mexico was a nation with a population exceeding eight million people, and thirty thousand of them lived in Texas, virtually all of which were located between the Sabine and Guadalupe Rivers (see Figure 1.) The *alcalde* of San Felipe called for a "mass meeting" to discuss the political future of Texas. People wanted to go on record *against* the rumor that Texas sought independence from Mexico, but the concept of a mass meeting to intelligently discuss principles without coming to blows was an unknown and impossible concept in the Mexican culture.

Nonetheless, in October of that year, delegates met in Bastrop from everywhere except the largely Mexican population of San Antonio de Béxar. It was found that the delegates were well balanced between a conservative party that did not favor separation from Mexico, and a radical party that secretly favored independence though they openly avowed to the contrary. Stephen Austin was the soul and leader of the conservatives, and William Wharton was leader of the more radical element. Austin was elected president.

The convention voted to petition the government to become a separate Mexican state by a margin of three to one, but this was never actually presented to the people for ratification. It should be noted that 1827 provisions in the Mexican Constitution of Coahuila y Texas (the state that included the Texas territory) allowed for Texas to become its own state with its own government. In fact those provisions declared that as soon as Texas should be in a condition to form a state it should make a declaration to that effect to Congress for further action. Even so, distrust of the Anglo-Texans had been growing in the Mexican national government which caused the government to view many acts and actions by the Texans through the lens of treason. All the while, much of the Anglo population remained somewhat oblivious to the changing sentiment. And among the more radical Texan elements, distrust of the Mexican Government simmered over fears of losing their constitutionally-guaranteed civil rights, freedoms, and political representation.

Austin Goes to Mexico

The question of separate statehood arose again in 1833 and 1834. A second convention met in 1833 when a proposed State Constitution under the Mexican flag was actually drafted. Austin would soon travel to Mexico City to present this petition for statehood to Congress. The document was couched in the most respectful and genteel terms—its language was carefully selected and guarded. Mexican authorities, however, and even some Mexican citizens in Texas, viewed this respectful petition as treason and/or a declaration of war. Such was the opinion of the Mexican governor of Coahuila y Texas. Against Austin's better judgment, but because he knew that he alone would have any chance of success, Austin personally traveled to Mexico City to present the petition to Congress, arriving in June 1833. He was thirty-nine years old, and he paid for the trip out of his own pocket.

Austin labored at this for six months, succeeding only in getting the Decree of 1830, which prohibited immigration from the U.S., revoked. While remarkable that he accomplished even this, he was not received warmly and was indeed distrusted, departing the City in December 1833.

While leaving, he wrote a letter to the *ayuntamiento* in San Antonio de Béxar encouraging it and all municipalities to join the push for Texas to become its own state in the Mexican Federation. He encouraged the *ayuntamientos* to communicate with each other for the purpose of organizing a functional state-level government for Texas even if the federal government refused to consent to statehood. In proposing a state government be formed, Austin was trying everything he could to avoid an outright revolt of the Anglo citizens who were increasingly frustrated with the lack of effective government in their territory. The letter found its way to authorities in Mexico City who had him arrested for treason on January 3, 1834, while on his way back to Texas. He was thrown into solitary confinement in a windowless dungeon measuring thirteen-by-sixteen-feet that was left over from the Spanish Inquisition. He would remain incarcerated until being released almost a year later in December 1834 after having never been formally charged and never given any explanation for his imprisonment. He was left to assume that it was due to the letter he had written to the *ayuntamientos*. During this time, he wrote,

> What a horrible punishment is solitary confinement, shut up in a dungeon with scarcely light to distinguish anything. If I were a criminal it would be one thing, but I am not one. I have been ensnared and precipitated, but my intentions were pure and correct.

And in another letter to his old friend Rafael Llanos, senator from Nuevo León, he lamented dreams disappointed and plans thwarted by the ignorance and prejudice of the Government.

During Austin's incarceration, a gloom was cast over the Texas settlements. The high hopes that his trip to Mexico City would successfully address their concerns and desires were dashed. People were afraid to express their opinions or take action for fear that such action would cost Austin his life. In the meantime every semblance of state government in Coahuila y Texas was falling apart. A civil war was brewing in Coahuila between two Mexican factions and anarchy prevailed. Texas now had no government except the local town councils, which provided enough of a framework to be functional for the industrious and orderly people of the colonies. But Texas had now gone from being woefully under-represented to being un-represented.

On October 5, 1834, in Mexico City, President Santa Anna called a council to discuss the state of affairs in Texas. Among those present were Lorenzo de Zavala, then a high-ranking Mexican official who would soon become a Texas patriot, and Stephen Austin, who was allowed out of prison to sit in the council. It was ultimately decreed that Texas would not become an independent Mexican state, and it was evident that the president's policy was to militarily occupy Texas in order to control the colonists and compel their subjection. Santa Anna would soon send a force of many thousands to Texas for this very purpose.

Austin was returned to his prison cell, and a garrison of troops arrived in San Antonio de Béxar under the leadership of General Martín Perfecto de Cós, who quickly issued arrest warrants for some of the more outspoken men in the colonies for "seditious utterances." These included Colonel William Travis, Lorenzo de Zavala, and others. Letters from General Cós talked of active plans to punish the colonies, and the militia movement began organizing everywhere in Texas. Few now doubted that war was coming, and wild rumors of Mexican invasion and Indian uprisings were rampant.

Gonzales

On October 2, 1835, the storm clouds over Texas broke when a small Mexican detachment from General Cós's army numbering about one hundred troops (Anglo estimates exaggerate this figure), under the command of

Lieutenant Francisco Castañeda, descended upon the settlement at Gonzales, about sixty miles east of San Antonio de Béxar, to confiscate a small cannon which the Mexican Government had furnished to the citizens four years earlier for defense against the Indians. Anticipating this attempt, 168 Texans had hurriedly gathered with no intention of surrendering it and under the "Come and Take It" flag (see Figure 9), advanced to within 350 yards of the Mexican detachment, shielded by a dense morning fog, and fired their cannon, refusing to give it up.

A parley was proposed by Mexican Commander Castañeda, who then met with Colonel John H. Moore, acting Commander of the Gonzales brigade. Castañeda demanded to know why the Texans had fired on them. Moore replied that Castañeda had made a demand on their cannon, and in case of refusal, intended to take it by force; that he was acting under the orders of the tyrant, Santa Anna, who had broken down and trampled underfoot the State and Federal Constitutions in Mexico; and that the Texans were determined to fight for their rights under the Constitution of 1824 until the last gasp. Castañeda replied that he himself was a republican and that two-thirds of the Mexican nation was also, but that the people of Texas were bound to submit to the new government. He added that he did not want to fight the Texans. Colonel Moore then demanded Castañeda's surrender, along with the troops under his command, or that he join the Texans' cause. Castañeda indicated that he would obey orders, and the parlay ended.

A short skirmish ensued in which a few Mexicans were killed but no Texans. The Mexican detachment instantly retreated and took flight for San Antonio de Béxar. As insignificant as it was in the matter of bloodshed, it was to the Texans what the affair at Lexington was to the American Colonies. The first shots of the Revolution had been fired.

In Mexico that very same month, the Federal Constitution of 1824 was scrapped in favor of a dictatorial form a government. Santa Anna, who had once championed that Constitution and the freedoms it guaranteed, declared himself dictator and published to the world that the Federal Government and Constitution of 1824 were no more. Even though a majority of the Mexican population was opposed to Santa Anna's consolidation of power, they were ultimately powerless to resist his might.

A Solemn Realization

What course should the people of Texas now pursue? Should they battle alone for the reestablishment of the Federal Constitution after almost every voice in its favor had been silenced in Mexico? Should they consent to being a remote territorial appendage to the central government governed by a military officer and a bishop? Should they lay down their arms and hope that some favorable change in Mexico would lead to the rise of peace and security? The settlers knew full well that the government of Mexico sought to regain its lost laurels and punish the rebels. What possible consistent course was left but to declare full independence and go to war? Many of the more intelligent settlers now saw this last option as the only alternative.

A month prior, following his two-and-a-half-year absence from Texas, Stephen Austin arrived in Brazoria, Texas, on September 1, 1835. He addressed over one thousand people there in a speech a week later:

> I left Texas in April 1833 as the public agent of the people, for the purpose of applying for the admission of this country into the Mexican confederation as a state separate from Coahuila. This application was based upon the constitutional and vested rights of Texas . . . I was arrested and have suffered a long persecution and imprisonment . . . I have never, in any manner, agreed to anything, or admitted anything, that would compromise the constitutional or vested rights of Texas. These rights belong to the people and can only be surrendered by them.
>
> I fully hoped to find Texas at peace . . . but regret to find it . . . disorganized, all in anarchy, and threatened with immediate hostilities . . . it is a great misfortune, but it is one which has not been produced by any acts of the people of this country; on the contrary, it is the natural and inevitable consequence of the revolution that had spread all over Mexico, and the imprudent and impolitic measures of both the state and general governments with respect to Texas.
>
> The revolution in Mexico is drawing to a close. The object is to change the form of government, destroy the

Federal Constitution of 1824, and establish a central or consolidated government ... An important question now presents itself to the people of this country ... Will this act annihilate all the rights of Texas, and subject this country to the uncontrolled and unlimited dictation of the new government?

This country [the Texas territory] is now in anarchy, threatened with hostilities, armed vessels are capturing everything they can catch on the coast, and acts of piracy are said to be committed under cover of the Mexican flag. Can this state of things exist without precipitating the country into a war? I think it cannot, and therefore believe that it is our bounden and solemn duty as Mexicans and as Texans to represent the evils [to the national government] that are likely to result from this mistaken and most impolitic policy.

My friends, I can truly say that no one has been, or is now, more anxious than myself to keep trouble away from this country. No one has been, or now is, more faithful to his duty as a Mexican citizen ... Texas needs peace and a local government; its inhabitants are farmers, and they need a calm and quiet life. But how can I, or anyone, remain indifferent when our rights, our all, appear to be in jeopardy, and when it is our duty, as well as our obligation as good Mexican citizens, to express our opinions on the present state of things and to represent our situation to the government? It is impossible ... What are we to do? ... Let all personalities or divisions, or excitements, or passion, or violence be banished from among us. Let a general

> consultation of the people of Texas be convened as speedily as possible . . . and let them decide what representations ought to be made to the general government, and what ought to be done in future.

And he toasted to the constitutional rights, security, and peace of Texas.

Only eleven days later, on September 19, Austin wrote to his friend, W. D. C. Hall:

> War is upon us and there is no remedy . . . the people must unconditionally submit to whatever the Government chooses to do for them . . . This is impossible; we had better leave the country at once, for we should be . . . without any rights or guaranties [*sic*] of any kind. I therefore think that war is inevitable; we must prepare . . .

Sugar-Plums and Honey

Around the same time, Lorenzo de Zavala arrived at San Felipe de Austin and took his seat as chairman of the Committee of Safety in that jurisdiction. These committees had been created to fill in for the increasingly nonexistent state and local governments. De Zavala, the high-ranking Mexican government official, had fled to Texas in the face of rising tyranny in Mexico. He advised the citizens there of the history of Mexico and the character and motives of the men in power. He represented that the military was the regulating power in Mexico, not the Constitution; that the situation in Mexico was one of confusion and disorder; that Santa Anna had between fifteen and twenty thousand soldiers at his disposal and knew no law but that of the sword and violence and had put down all the constitutional and civil authorities; and that he believed that the civil and political rights of the citizen had been destroyed. His thoughts were instrumental in directing public sentiment among the settlers.

A circular was written by Austin on October 3 in his capacity as a member of the Committee of Safety. Excerpts from it follow and show the prevailing sentiment. This would be the last official act by Austin before the war commenced:

> All are aware of the present movements of volunteers towards the western frontiers ... Information ... had been received here as to the marching of [Mexican] soldiers from Béxar ... The object appears to be the apprehension of certain citizens, among whom Don Lorenzo de Zavala, now a citizen of Texas, was particularly designated and aimed at. This gentleman had come to Texas, as ... an asylum from the persecution of the present administration of Mexico. His offense we know not, except that he is the known friend of free institutions ... The authorities of Texas have been arbitrarily required by a military mandate to surrender [him] into the hands of General Cós, who ... issued an order ... to march into the colonies and take him, at the risk of losing all the force he should employ. The issuing of [this order] is at once an open outrage upon the civil authorities of Texas, and upon the Constitution. But what is of most

importance . . . show[s] us all what kind of government the present reformers in Mexico are aiming to subject us to—which is the government of the bayonet, and the regulation of all the affairs of Texas by military power, regardless of the Constitution . . .

A disastrous and ruinous civil war [in Mexico] was kindled in 1832, by means of an insurrection against the Bustamente administration, and General Santa Anna was placed at its head. The avowed object of this insurrection was to protect the federal system, and sustain the Constitution of 1824 . . . On this principle the people of Texas supported General Santa Anna to defend the Constitution of 1824, and the federal system. This general was enthusiastically supported by every liberal and free Mexican, and by the friends of the federal system in every part of the nation . . . He became the man of the people—the protector of the federal system . . . How has he used this power? . . . Let the military despotism now enthroned in Mexico upon the ruins of the federal system—let the friends of this system, who are now groaning in prisons or wandering in exile—let the Constitution of 1824, which still raises its dying voice from beneath the feet of military usurpation—let the free and impartial in Mexico and in the whole civilized world give the reply. They all say, he used it to destroy what he avowed he had taken up arms to protect . . . This . . . party is now governing in Mexico, and they say to the people of Texas, in the language of friendship and persuasion—in that of sugar-plums and honey, that in the new Constitution, or central government ... guarantees shall be given to the people of Texas, their rights shall be protected and secured, and they are told that the government expects from their "docility" a submission to all reforms ...

What is here meant by "reforming" the Constitution of 1824, may be clearly deduced by the "reform" of the militia made by this same general Congress. This "reform" reduced the militia of the states to one militia-man for every five hundred inhabitants, and disarmed all the rest ... In fact, "reform" means destruction.

From this condensed view of the past, let every impartial man judge for himself what degree of faith or credit ought to be given to the professions of the present government of Mexico, and ask himself whether a subtle poison may not be concealed in the sugar-plums, or a sting in the honey, that is now offered to the "docile" people of Texas.

Now, if the present government of Mexico is sincere in its professions of liberal guarantees for Texas, why all this preparation for a military invasion?

... Will the people of Texas submit to all this? Let each man study the subject, and answer for himself. If he will submit, let him go to the military power and prostrate himself. If he will not submit, let him give his answer from the mouth of his rifle! ...

Interestingly, within a few days of this circular, an incident occurred between Stephen Austin and William Wharton that further demonstrated how Austin's views on Texas' relationship with Mexico had come full circle.

The two had been estranged for years and were not on speaking terms, being leaders of the opposing conservative and radical political elements, with deep disagreements about policy for Texas.

Wharton and a friend had reached a log house in Gonzales where they were going to spend the night and were told that Austin had arrived a few hours before. With permission, Wharton entered Austin's room to offer reconciliation and found him laying on a blanket, utterly exhausted from the long day's ride in the rain, his face thin and pale. Austin was glad to forget all differences and make amends with Wharton now that he had become convinced the political powers in Mexico could no longer be trusted. The buoyant young man who fourteen years before had ridden to San Antonio de Béxar to begin his colonial enterprise was, at forty-one, a broken and dying man, who in a dismal voice bemoaned the plight of "poor Texas." He would die fourteen months later in December 1836, only eight months after his beloved Texas had won its independence.

The Federal Army

The next day Austin was elected Commander-in-Chief of the "Federal Army" by the gathering patriots. He had no military experience, his health was bad, and he was by no means an ideal military commander, though he lacked neither courage nor firmness. His "army" of militia men totaled six hundred.

Entrepreneur and empresario Ben Milam, who would soon become the hero of the Battle of Béxar, was in Mexico when the Constitution of 1824 was annulled by Santa Anna in October 1835. He was arrested as a traitor while attempting to return to Texas. He apparently bribed the prison guards who were sympathetic to the republicans and the Texans' cause and escaped. While on his way back to Texas he engaged in a scouting mission along the Rio Grande.

Noah Smithwick, a young man who was one of the volunteers serving in the Texas army, recalled of him:

> Colonel Milam joined us at Gonzales. He had recently escaped a Mexican prison and his wardrobe was much depleted. He was more than six feet [tall] and his pantaloons and sleeves were far too short for his stature.

Smithwick went on to describe the dress of his fellow volunteer soldiers:

> Buckskin breeches were the nearest approach to uniform, and they were of every variety and complexion—some too short, others too long. Here a broad brimmed sombrero overshadowed a military cap and a tall bee gum [an early cowboy hat with a small brim and formless round top] would ride along with a coonskin cap with tail hanging down behind as all well-regulated tails should do . . . In lieu of canteens each soldier carried a Spanish gourd. So, with the old cannon flag flying and the artillery [one lone cannon] mounted on a wooden wheeled wagon driven by teams of oxen, we filed out of Gonzales and took up our march on to San Antonio. At Cibola [*sic*] Creek, Sam Houston came up with us. It was my first sight of him.

Indeed this "army" should be more accurately labeled a militia, but only if that word can be used to describe an assembly of armed men who were largely without any training whatsoever, other than the personal skills of hunting and protection, and who, for the most part, were under no compulsion to serve.

The Texan militia was, by any account, woefully under-equipped, as described on October 17 in the San Felipe *Telegraph*, a patriotic gazette:

> Texas patriotism.— It is gratifying to witness the public spirit which everywhere manifests itself in the service of the country. We know one man who has taken the leaden pipes out of his aqueduct to furnish ammunition for the army; and a number of others who have melted up their clock weights . . . for the same purpose. Even the ladies, bless their souls, volunteer their services in moulding [*sic*] and patching bullets, making cartridges . . .

Indeed, the people who gathered to defend their lives, land, and ideals were only an army in the academic sense. They were farmers and adventurers, paid and fed on promises, who only had their personal guns used to tame the land; and only a very few had any military experience, let alone the discipline to act cohesively.

Nonetheless, this Texan militia under the command of General Austin arrived on the outskirts of San Antonio de Béxar in late October 1835 having increased in size to about seven hundred men. There was a difference of opinion as to whether the city, or more particularly General Cós and the more than one thousand soldiers who occupied it, should be stormed immediately, or if the Texan militia should go home and recess in favor of a spring campaign.

The Battle of Concepción

Austin camped his militia and waited for reinforcements that he hoped would arrive. Growing tired of waiting after a week, he detached Colonels James Fannin and James Bowie with ninety-two men to find a suitable location to move his militia closer to the enemy, setting out on the evening of October 27, and arriving at Mission Concepción (one mile south of the town of San Antonio de Béxar) before dawn the next day. Mexican General Cós had been observing the movements of the Texan detachment and determined it to be small compared to his force. Cós made the tactical decision to attack that very morning before Austin could arrive with his main force. Cós hoped that a decisive victory over this detachment would cause panic among the larger Texan force and delay any operation against him long enough for Santa Anna to arrive with his even larger army.

At 8:00 A.M. on October 28 as a dense fog lifted, the Texans found themselves surrounded, unable to communicate with the main body of Austin's militia. Shots were fired by the Mexicans first, and immediately both sides were fully engaged. The Texans with superior marksmanship quickly gained the upper hand, silenced the Mexican cannon, and caused a hasty retreat in which the Mexicans abandoned the cannon to the Texans. Outnumbered four-to-one, the Texans soundly defeated the Mexicans with the loss of only one man and none injured. Mexican losses are said to have been seventy-seven with more injured. If Gonzales was Texas' Lexington, Concepción was its Bunker Hill, proving that the Texans could stand up against the superior military of the Mexican nation.

Buoyed by the victory in the Battle of Concepción, spirits in the Texan ranks soared, but intelligence suggested the Mexican army in San Antonio de Béxar was strengthening. And Austin did not dare risk attacking the entrenched force there.

Meanwhile a third Consultation was organized at San Felipe in October/November 1835 to discuss next steps—whether to make one last final effort to acknowledge loyalty to the Mexican Constitution of 1824, or to declare independence. The Whartons, William and his brother John, led the fight for an immediate declaration of independence, while Sam Houston and other older men urged a last stand for the Federal Constitution. But Texas would soon be undeceived in this vain hope, and when the next convention would meet the following March, a declaration of independence would be adopted in the opening hours.

In this present consultation, Stephen Austin and William Wharton were chosen commissioners to the United States and urged to proceed there at once to use every means necessary to arouse sympathy and procure assistance. Thus on November 24, 1835, Austin and Wharton, old political enemies turned allies, left the militia to accept the mission to the United States. Edward Burleson was chosen as Austin's replacement, and while he was not a great commander, he was a great fighter, living to a ripe old age after surviving thirty-two battles.

On November 29, the General Council passed an ordinance declaring the creation of a flag with instructions that "1824" replace the eagle in the center of the Mexican flag. This was intended as a sharp rebuke to Mexico that the Texans had been denied their rights as Mexican citizens under the Mexican Constitution of that year (see Figure 8).

And this is how we find the state of affairs in Texas at the end of November 1835. The Constitution had been cancelled; Austin had left Texas on his mission to the United States; the all-volunteer Texan militia under dubious leadership was unable to decide if the next move should be to fight or go home, even while it camped out around San Antonio de Béxar in a siege of the Mexican forces under General Cós; and leadership was clinging to the hope of upholding the Mexican Constitution of 1824, even after every Mexican state had succumbed to the dictator who was systematically putting down all opposition to his declared authority.

IV. THE BATTLE OF BÉXAR AND THE CONVENTION OF 1836

Intelligence had confirmed that General Cós's Mexican army at San Antonio de Béxar was preparing for a war of extermination against the people of Texas even while the Texans who were camped on the outskirts of town remained indecisive about their next move.

Enter Ben Milam on December 4, 1835, as he returned from his Mexican imprisonment. He would fill the leadership vacuum and forever become known as the hero of the Battle of Béxar. He was a man of wonderful personality, tall, and powerful. He walked among this seven hundred-man militia of countrymen hearing their quibbling. Without a council of war, he boldly asked, "Who will go into San Antonio with old Ben Milam?" Having thus advertised the excursion, he was quick to capitalize on the enthusiasm it produced. The Battle of Béxar soon began and raged for six days, beginning as house-to-house combat in the town and ending in a Mexican surrender at the site we now know as the Alamo. The battle resulted in the complete capitulation of the Mexican Army. Ben Milam was killed on day three and was buried where he fell.

The initial battle which occurred in the town was characterized by sniper fire from rooftops and windows until the Texans conceived the idea of breaking through the common walls of the row houses until they were in control of an entire row. One participant recalled,

> We went through the old adobe and picket houses . . . using battering-rams made out of logs ten or twelve feet long. The stout men would take hold of the logs and swing them awhile . . . punching holes in the walls through which we passed. How the women and children would yell when we knocked the holes in the walls and went in!

The Texans slowly ground their way towards control of the town, eventually putting the Mexicans in an untenable situation. This culminated in General Cós retreating under the cover of darkness into the Alamo.

The general's withdrawal from the town caused great panic among the citizens, mass desertion of his soldiers, and insubordination of many that remained. In fact, the Texans had learned from a deserter that among the thirteen-hundred-strong Mexican army stationed there, many dissatisfied, republican-minded troops under Cós's command were opposed to Santa Anna's centralized government. The Texans took advantage of this information in their plan of attack. Panicked women and their children, thinking the Mexican withdrawal to the Alamo was a rout, fled there seeking safety.

General Cós found himself in charge of a mass confusion of soldiers and citizens, and he had no choice but to surrender. Terms of the surrender included that the

Mexican Army would leave Texas; that they would not oppose the reestablishment of the Constitution of 1824; a promise from General Cós never to set foot on Texas soil again (which he would soon break at San Jacinto); and that all war materials would be conveyed to the Texans. The victors received twenty-one pieces of artillery and five hundred muskets with ammunition. In less than three months, these munitions would be used by the defenders of the Alamo in their defense of Texas.

Following Cós's humiliating defeat and subsequent retreat south of the Rio Grande River along with the army under his command, no active Mexican soldiers remained on Texas soil.

With the defeat of the Mexican army at the Battle of Béxar, the volunteer militia took leave for their homes and left only a small detachment of approximately 150 men at Béxar. It was widely expected that a large Mexican army would organize for invasion, but the settlers knew that would take time to plan and execute. Sam Houston, though arguably the most accomplished man in Texas, having served as a congressman from Tennessee and the state's governor prior to settling in east Texas at the end of 1832, had military experience but no formal military training. Nonetheless, he had now been selected as Commander-in-Chief of the Texas army. This high-sounding phrase was a mockery, because Texas had no functional government, no war chest, no army in the traditional sense, no credit, and no plan for concerted defensive action.

General Houston issued a proclamation from Washington-on-the-Brazos on December 12 to rally the citizens to arms:

> CITIZENS OF TEXAS— ... Under the Republican constitution of Mexico, you were invited to Texas, then a wilderness. You have reclaimed and rendered it a cultivated country. You solemnly swore to support the Constitution and its laws ... In accordance with them, you have fought with the Liberals against those who sought to overthrow the Constitution, in 1832, when the present usurper was the champion of Liberal principles in Mexico. [Before Santa Anna morphed into a tyrannical dictator, he was the champion of the 1824 Constitution and "the man of the people"] ... You have realized the horrors of anarchy, and the dictation of military rule ... the agents you sent to Mexico have been imprisoned for years, without enjoying the right of trial according to law ... The [Mexican] Federation has been dissolved—the Constitution declared at an end, and Centralism has been established ... You remained loyal to the duty of citizens, with the hope that Liberty would not perish in the Republic of Mexico. But while you were fondly cherishing this hope, the Dictator required the surrender of the arms of the civic militia, that he might be able to establish on the ruins of the Constitution, a system of policy that would forever enslave the people of Mexico ... By the first of March next, we must meet the enemy with an

> army worthy of our cause ... Liberal Mexicans will unite with us ... Let the brave rally to our standard.
>
> —SAM HOUSTON

Meanwhile, Colonel James Fannin, Dr. James Grant, Colonel Frank Johnson, and other visionary incompetents were planning invasions of Mexico by way of Matamoros with fewer than five hundred men and without sufficient means of transportation or supplies. Sam Houston was unable to exercise his authority over this militia but used these next several months to convene a series of conversations with the Indians whose attitude was a matter of concern at this point. Mexico had been agitating the bands of Indian warriors all along the frontier, and those Indians could have swept through the settlements in a week. Altogether Houston held thirteen councils with them, and he alone was uniquely qualified to engage them. He had run away from home as a boy and lived among the Cherokee Indians. He had learned to speak the language, adopted their customs and dress, and had become a legal citizen of the Cherokee Nation. As a council member, he was considered a chief. He regarded the Cherokee as his family, and his Indian name was *Colonneh,* meaning "the Raven." Later the Indians would nickname him "Big Drunk" for reasons you might imagine. Houston loved and was beloved by the Indians all of his life. To him, Texas owes a debt of gratitude that these warriors did not draw the bow against the patriots during the campaign of 1836.

The Convention of 1836

Against the backdrop of the assembling Mexican army—which would number approximately seventy-five hundred soldiers in the Texas territory—perhaps one hundred fifty men were holed up at the Alamo, supplied largely with the captured guns and artillery from the Battle of Béxar. Meanwhile, fewer than one thousand men would be recruited by Sam Houston to raise arms in the name of Freedom.

By now the General Council, which was the settlers' governing body, had fallen to pieces. It is hard to imagine darker prospects for the fledgling patriots. For the fourth time in Texas' brief history, a convention of all Texas met, this time at Washington-on-the-Brazos on March 1, 1836 (see Figure 5).

In the opening minutes of March 2, an already-drafted Declaration of Independence was motioned by General Houston and unanimously adopted. It was Houston's forty-third birthday. Two days later on March 4, Houston was again appointed Commander-in-Chief of the Federal Army, now under authority of the ad interim government. The following Sunday, March 6, Alamo courier John Smith arrived at the convention at about the same hour as the Alamo fell, bearing William Travis's final appeal letter, dated March 3. General Houston was there to receive Travis's plea for help just before he departed towards the west in a cold March rain. He was accompanied by an escort of two aids, a captain, and a boy. Under these auspices, he was sent to produce an army, defend a people, and birth a nation.

With independence declared and Houston on the way west towards Gonzales, the convention began its work on the new country's first constitution, our forefathers being firm believers in a written constitutional government. It would reflect the republican ideals of guaranteed freedoms found in the Mexican Constitution of 1824 and also in the Constitution of the United States. Even after its adoption, no one knew if it would ever be submitted to a general election of the people for ratification. There was, after all, a large military force bearing down upon them which was bent on extermination. Holding an election would be impossible. Until such time as an improbable military victory could be achieved and the Constitution ratified by a vote of the citizens, an ad interim government was provided, with David Burnet chosen as president, and the Mexican/Spaniard Lorenzo de Zavala chosen as vice president. The convention finished its work on the night of March 17, hastened by a rumor that the Mexican Army was near, and having received word by courier on the fifteenth that the Alamo had fallen nine days before. (For a reference map of Texas and Mexican troop movements, see Figure 2.)

Among other things, the Declaration of Independence cited the following:

> When a government has ceased to protect the lives, liberty and property of the people, from whom all its legitimate powers are derived, and ... becomes an instrument in the hands of evil rulers for their oppression; when the federal republican constitution of their

country, which they have sworn to support, no longer has a substantial existence, and the whole nature of their government has been forcibly changed, without their consent, from a restricted federative republic ... to a consolidated military despotism ... and mercenary armies sent forth to enforce a new government upon them at the point of the bayonet ... When, anarchy prevails, and civil society is dissolved ... to abolish such government and create another in its stead ...

The Mexican Government, by its colonization laws, invited and induced the Anglo-American population of Texas to colonize its wilderness under the pledged faith of a written constitution ...

In this expectation they have been cruelly disappointed, in as much as the Mexican nation has acquiesced in the late changes made in the government by General Antonio López de Santa Anna, who, having overturned the Constitution of his country, now offers us the cruel alternatives either to abandon our homes, acquired by so many privations, or submit to the most intolerable tyranny ... and we have petitioned in the humblest terms for an establishment of a separate state government, which was without just cause, contemptuously rejected.

It has failed and refused to secure on a firm basis the right to trial by jury.

... The military commandants stationed among us ... exercise arbitrary acts of oppression and tyranny ...

It has dissolved by force the arms of the State Congress of Coahuila y Texas ...

> It has demanded us to deliver up our arms, which are essential to our defense—The rightful property of free men . . .
>
> It has invaded our country both by sea and by land, with the intent to lay waste our territory and drive us from our homes, and has now a large mercenary army advancing to carry on against us a war of extermination.
>
> We are, therefore, forced to the melancholy conclusion that the Mexican people have acquiesced in the destruction of their liberty and the substitution therefor [*sic*] of a military government; that they are unfit to be free and incapable of self-government.

Of the fifty-eight signers of the Texas Declaration of Independence, fully forty of them were under forty years old. Most of them were from the southern United States; two were native Texans from Béxar; and they also included an Englishman, a Canadian, a Spaniard, an Irishman, and a Scotsman.

V. THE ALAMO

The old Spanish Mission fortress we know as the Alamo was founded in 1718 by Franciscan friars as part of Spain's attempt to export Christianity and civilization to the indigenous people in the New World. Named Mission Valero, it moved to its present location on the San Antonio River just east of the San Antonio de Béxar settlement in 1724. The surviving stone structures we see today began construction in 1744. It was originally intended to serve its mission purpose for about ten years; it was not, however, decommissioned or secularized until 1793 when it was divided up among the remaining residents. Adjoining the chapel was a stone walled enclosure of about two city blocks which had been erected as a protection against Indian raids. Although substantial, the Alamo was never intended to be a military fortress from which to fight invading armies, much less armies with artillery.

In January 1836, following the Texans' victory over the Mexican army in the Battle of Béxar one month prior, most Texans had gone home, leaving Colonel James C. Neill in nominal charge of the Alamo garrison now totaling around eighty-six men. The Texas victory had left numerous guns and artillery in the Mission which the defenders would use in their coming fight. All of Texas knew that a large Mexican army was being formed to march upon Texas, and specifically San Antonio de Béxar—its largest town—and rumors of the army's approach were rampant. Henry Smith, who had been named Provisional Governor of the proposed separate Mexican state of Texas in the November 1835 Consultation, wrote letters attempting to get reinforcements to the Alamo, but he was not supported by the General Council, which was busy authorizing several individuals for haphazard invasions of Mexico.

Smith is widely recognized as the first American-born governor of Texas, although at the time Texas was still part of Mexico and not even a standalone state. Independence had not yet been declared when he was named governor—thus the "provisional" label. The General Council and governor each attempted to assume the roles of governance during this period given that the Mexican state and national governments had become non-existent. All the while, they wrestled with the decision to declare independence or to pursue individual statehood under the Mexican flag. Smith would serve in this capacity for only a few months until the provisional government was replaced with an ad interim government following the March 2 declaration of independence. The relationship between Smith and the General Council became dysfunctional within a few weeks and ushered in attempts by the General Council to impeach Smith, even while he attempted to disband the Council. In the madness of impending war, all government effectively collapsed.

Meanwhile James Fannin, James Grant, and Frank Johnson had planned their nonsensical invasions of Mexico. Chaos reigned. History suggests that no man had any functional vision to address the coming war except for Sam Houston, who at this juncture had no army and few prospects of any. Houston had ordered James Bowie to destroy the Alamo on December 15 and again on January 17, after which he was to retreat east with his garrison across the Guadalupe River in an effort to consolidate forces. Houston knew that fighting to protect a fixed asset such as the Alamo was futile in the face of a large invading army. Houston's orders were ignored both times by Bowie who had just defeated a larger Mexican force under General Cós at the Battle of Concepción and had done so without the benefit of a fortress. Bowie was feeling that his Texans were invincible, but he did not understand that his recent victory was over a detachment commanded by a very poor military leader—Cós. It is widely held that Cós was in this position of leadership because he was Santa Anna's brother-in-law, but definitive evidence of that relationship has yet to be presented.

Likewise, General Houston had urged Fannin with his five hundred men to retreat to Victoria, but Fannin had refused to recognize the Commander-in-Chief's authority. Houston understood the only hope this fledgling nation had was to rally the citizens once again, amass more volunteers while retreating east, and hope to find some tactical advantage in the woods of east Texas.

In mid-February Colonel David Crockett arrived at San Antonio de Béxar from Tennessee, having become enamored with Texas. After having lost a re-election bid to Congress, and convinced that it was stolen with bribed votes, he famously proclaimed to his constituents, "You may all go to Hell. I am going to Texas." And indeed, he did. With plans to insert himself into the freedom fight, he headed straight for San Antonio de Béxar and the Alamo.

Crockett kept a detailed journal from which we know much of the goings-on inside the Alamo prior to its fall. After the battle the journal was found in his baggage by Mexican General Castrillón's servant. Castrillón subsequently died in the Battle of San Jacinto, and the journal was retrieved from his luggage by Charles Beale, to be preserved for posterity. In it Crockett muses,

> And this is the way the Alamo came into our possession [having just described the Battle of Béxar]; but the way we shall maintain our possession of it will be a subject for the future historian to record, or my name's not Crockett.— I wish I may be shot if I don't go ahead to the last.

And,

> . . . if there is anything in this world particularly worth living for, it is freedom; anything that would render death to a brave man particularly pleasant, it is freedom.

He would soon be granted his "particularly pleasant" wish.

Crockett was a man of high ideals, intellect, and was quite a character. In his first journal entry upon arriving at the Alamo, Crockett recorded on February 19,

> We are all in high spirits, though we are rather short of provisions, for men who have appetites that could digest anything but oppression; but no matter, we have a prospect of soon getting our bellies full of fighting, and that is victuals and drink to a true patriot any day.

Early in the morning on February 23, 1836, Colonel William Barrett Travis—who had been appointed commandant of the Alamo garrison by Governor Smith, but who shared leadership with troop-elected James Bowie—reported the Mexican army in sight one mile away, camped at the main plaza of San Antonio de Béxar. Crockett records,

> That afternoon a messenger was sent from the enemy to Col. Travis demanding an unconditional and absolute surrender of the garrison, threatening to put every man to the sword in case of refusal. The only answer he received was a cannon shot.

The siege of the Alamo and the "thirteen days to glory," as this immortal resistance became known, had begun.

THIRTEEN DAYS TO GLORY

Travis appears to have been careless about keeping abreast of the movements of the enemy and was apparently unprepared and short of provisions when the enemy presented itself. It was the pervading opinion among Texans, after vanquishing the Mexican army in the Battle of Béxar, that Santa Anna would not be able to rally an army for invasion until mid-summer. Santa Anna, on the other hand, felt his power was deeply threatened. He force-marched his army by extraordinary means back to Texas, arriving in February. Many soldiers died along the way due to exhaustion.

Mexican General Vicente Filísola described the wake of this fast-moving march as a

> wreckage of carts, harness boxes, skeletons of oxen, mules, and horses, piles of rubble . . . and small crosses and rough fences [grave markers] trodden underfoot by the soldiers marching over the graves of their less fortunate companions who had died . . .

Santa Anna was drunk with his own ambition and "the vertigo of his own speed," while the suffering of the people doing his bidding met with no sympathy whatsoever from their leader.

This early and unexpected appearance by the Mexican army accounts for the fact that the Texans were not prepared. Travis made his famous appeal for help in a letter dated the next day, here in its entirety:

Commandancy of the Alamo
Béxar, Feby. 24th/ 1836

To the People of Texas & all Americans in the World-
Fellow Citizens & Compatriots—

I am besieged by a thousand or more of the Mexicans under Santa Anna— I have sustained a continual bombardment & cannonade for 24 hours & have not lost a man— The enemy has demanded a surrender at discretion, otherwise, the garrison are to be put to the sword, if the fort is taken— I have answered their demand with a cannon shot, and our flag still waves proudly from our walls— I shall never surrender or retreat Then, [underlining in the original] I call upon you in the name of Liberty, of patriotism and everything dear to the American character, to come to our aid, with all dispatch—The enemy is receiving reinforcements daily & will no doubt increase to three or four thousand in four or five days. If this call is neglected, I am determined to sustain myself as long as possible & die like a soldier who never forgets what is due to his own honor & that of his country—

Victory or Death

WILLIAM BARRET TRAVIS

LT. COL. COM[MAN]D[AN]T

P. S. The Lord is on our side—When the enemy appeared in sight, we had not three bushels of corn—We have since found in deserted houses 80 or 90 bushels and got into the walls 20 or 30 head of beeves—TRAVIS

In this letter Colonel Travis appealed to the shared love of Freedom that he and the Texas settlers, now revolutionaries, shared with their American sympathizers. Since Mexico had proven untrustworthy, he turned to Americans in his appeal for help because he knew they shared a similar worldview that would be sympathetic to the Texan cause. The American Revolution, after all, was only sixty years prior and those wounds still lingered.

A. A. Parker, in his observations of the inhabitants of Texas at this time, says

> [the people having] buckled on their armor in a contest for liberty and independence, it is natural that Americans should feel a strong sympathy on their behalf. The sons of freedom can never be indifferent and unconcerned, in a struggle between liberty and despotic power, however remote the theatre of action; but when such a war is waged by their neighbors and friends, and Freedom the prize to be lost or won, the deep feeling pervading American breasts, cannot be suppressed.

The simple translation: The love of freedom breeds a kindred spirit that will come to the aid of other freedom-lovers whose freedom is being attacked.

Back in the Alamo, Crockett recalls of Colonel James Bowie:

> I was introduced to him by Colonel Travis, and he gave me a friendly welcome ... While we were conversing, he had occasion to draw his famous knife to cut a strap, and I wish I may be shot if the bare sight of it wasn't enough to give a man of a squeamish stomach the cholic, especially before breakfast.

He goes on to describe Bowie as "worth a dozen common men in a situation like ours." Unfortunately Bowie, a fierce fighter beloved by his men, fell gravely sick early in the siege and would not recover.

Crockett's journal gives us an amazing firsthand account of the battle as it unfolded. On February 27, the fifth day of the siege, he recorded:

> The cannonading began early this morning, and ten bombs were thrown into the fort, but fortunately exploded without doing any mischief ... Provisions are becoming scarce, and the enemy are endeavoring to cut off our water ... If they attempt to stop our grog in that manner, let them look out, for we shall become too wrathy for our shirts to hold us.

Crockett, February 28 (Day 6 of the siege)—

> Last night our hunters brought in some corn and hogs and had a brush with a scout from the enemy ... and got in without injury. They bring accounts that the settlers are flying in all quarters, in dismay, leaving their

> possessions to the mercy of the ruthless invader, who is literally engaged in a war of extermination. Slaughter is indiscriminate, sparing neither sex, age or condition. Buildings have been burned down; farms laid waste . . .

On February 29 (Day 7 of the siege), Crockett records a compelling story about a rude awakening he received from the enemy that morning. In it, he mentions a companion he had nicknamed Thimblerig. The man was drifting through life as a con-man when Crockett encountered him on his way to Texas from Tennessee. The man used thimbles to play the shell game and con people out of their money. Crockett had persuaded him to stand for something bigger than his current life. Thimblerig bought in to this higher calling and accompanied Crockett to the Alamo where he died as a patriot standing for Freedom's cause.

> . . . I had a little sport this morning before breakfast. The enemy had placed a piece of ordinance within gun-shot of the fort during the night, and the first thing this morning, they commenced a brisk cannonade, point blank, against the spot where I was snoring. I turned out pretty smart and mounted the rampart. The gun was charged again, and a fellow stepped forth to touch her off, but before he could apply the match, I let him have it, and he keeled over. A second stepped up, snatched the match from the hand of the dying man, but Thimblerig, who had followed me, handed me his rifle, and the next instant the Mexican was

stretched on the earth beside the first. A third came up to the cannon, my companion handed me another gun, and I fixed him off in a like manner. A fourth, then a fifth, seized the match, who both met with the same fate, and then the whole party gave it up as a bad job, and hurried off to the camp. I came down, took my bitters, and went to breakfast. Thimblerig told me that the place from which I had been firing was one of the snuggest stands in the whole fort, for he never failed picking off two or three stragglers before breakfast, when perched up there.

Crockett, March 1 (Day 8 of the siege)—

The enemy's forces have been increasing in numbers daily, notwithstanding, they have already lost about three hundred men in the several assaults they have made upon us . . . Col. Bowie's illness still continues, but he manages to crawl from his bed every day, that his comrades may see him. His presence alone is a tower of strength.— The enemy becomes more daring as his numbers increase.

Crockett, March 2 (Day 9 of the siege)—

This day the delegates meet in general convention, at the town of Washington, to frame our Declaration of Independence. *That the sacred instrument may never be trampled on by the children of those who have freely shed their blood to establish it, is the sincere wish of*

> *David Crockett* [emphasis added]. Universal independence is an almighty idea, far too extensive for some brains to comprehend.

> Crockett, March 3 (Day 10 of the siege)—

> We have given over all hope of receiving assistance from Goliad or Refugio. Colonel Travis harangued the garrison, and concluded by exhorting them, in case the enemy should carry the fort, to fight to the last gasp, and render their victory even more serious to them than to us. This was followed by three cheers.

> Crockett, March 4 (Day 11 of the siege)—

> Shells have been falling into the fort like hail during the day, but without effect.

> Crockett, March 5 (Day 12 of the siege)—

> Pop, pop, pop! Bom, bom, bom! throughout the day.— No time for memorandums now.— Go ahead!— Liberty and independence forever!

Here Crockett's diary falls silent, never to be resumed.

In the early morning of March 1, Captain Albert Martin along with thirty-one men came through the Mexican encirclement from Gonzales to take their place among the defenders. Two days later, James Bonham, who had been sent as a messenger to rally Fannin to come to the aid of the Alamo, rode back through the enemy lines to report no aid from that source would be coming. At about the same hour as Bonham came, Travis sent John Smith with the last of his bold appeals for help. That letter would reach the convention at Washington-on-the-Brazos on March 6 at the same hour as the Alamo fell, just before General Houston departed for Gonzales to rally an army to defend the people. Travis concluded this letter with,

> I look to the colonies alone for aid: unless it arrives soon, I shall have to fight the enemy on his own terms. I feel confident that the determined valor and desperate courage heretofore evinced by my men will not fail them in the last struggle; and although they may be sacrificed to the vengeance of a Gothic enemy, the victory will cost so dear, that it will be worse for him than a defeat. God and Texas! Victory or death!

And in a letter to a friend, the last correspondence Travis would write, he goes on to say,

> I am still here, in fine spirits . . . and I shall continue to hold [the Alamo] until I get relief from my countrymen, or I will perish in its defense . . . We had an action on the 25th in which we repulsed the enemy with considerable loss [to them]: on the night of the 25th, they made another attempt to charge us in the rear of the fort; but we received them gallantly, by a discharge of grapeshot [multiple small iron balls shot

from a cannon as opposed to a single projectile; the artillery equivalent to a shotgun] and musquetry [*sic*, musketry], they took to their scrapers immediately. They are now camped in entrenchments on all sides of us.

Let the Convention go on and make a declaration of Independence; and we will then understand, and the world will understand what we are fighting for . . . Under the flag of Independence, we are ready to peril our lives a hundred times a day, and to dare the monster who is fighting us under a blood-red flag, threatening to murder all prisoners and to make Texas a waste desert. I shall have to fight the enemy on his own terms; yet I am ready to do it, and if my countrymen do not rally to my relief, I am determined to perish in the defense of this place . . . My respects to all friends, and confusion to all enemies. God bless you.

The Fall of the Alamo

With 189 men plus some noncombatants inside the Alamo just before dawn on Sunday, March 6, and at least four thousand soldiers (some estimates are considerably higher, though the statement "at least 4000" appeared in the San Felipe *Telegraph* on March 24) outside the walls after having been reinforced by the 3rd Brigade, Mexican General Castrillón called for the silence to be broken with a bugle summoning the assault, while a band struck up *el degüello*—"the assassin's song." A half mile away, within sight of the defenders, a blood-red flag floated from the San Fernando de Béxar Church steeple (present-day San Fernando Cathedral in San Antonio), making it clear there would be no quarter given. At least three flags were flying over the Alamo that day, including the Two-Star Tricolor flag (see Figure 7) which was a modified Mexican flag with two stars replacing the eagle and representing two independent states of Coahuila and Texas. It was a reminder to Mexico that the patriots had first sought restoration of their rights and freedoms as Mexican citizens and also representation as a separate Mexican state, all of which had been denied. Under these circumstances the assault was engaged. Ninety minutes later, the last defender had fallen.

During the assault General Santa Anna remained camped to the south, safe from any gunfire, only coming forward after the battle was over. He would later write to his Secretary of War,

> . . . Among the corpses are those of Bowie and Travis, who styled themselves Colonels, and also that of Crockett . . . Nor will we hereafter suffer any foreigners, whatever their origins may be, to pollute our soil.

Crockett was one of six, it is believed, that survived the battle and surrendered under the promise of protection by General Castrillón, who by all accounts was a good and honorable man. When he surrendered, he was alone with the barrel of his shattered rifle in his right hand and a Bowie knife in his left hand. There was a gash across his forehead, while around him there was a barrier of about twenty Mexican soldiers lying pell-mell, dead and dying. Castrillón presented the six to Santa Anna, who had them immediately executed despite Castrillón's strong objections.

Bowie, who was still gravely sick, was killed in his bed and his body mutilated. The bodies of the Texans were stripped, thrown in a pile, and burned. Estimates as to the number of Mexican soldiers who died in the assault vary widely. It is believed that as many as six hundred were killed, but the actual figure may be far less.

The lives of as many as six inside the Alamo were spared. Some accounts vary as to the survivors, but they are thought to have included Mrs. Susanna Dickinson who was the wife of Lieutenant Almaron Dickinson, her eighteen-month-old daughter, as well as Mrs. Juana Navarro Alsbury of Béxar, another small child, one slave named Joe, and a Mexican woman. The defenders killed in the battle hailed from at least eleven southern states, six northern states, and seven foreign countries. The youngest defender was fifteen years old.

Travis and his followers could have escaped to Gonzales and retreated with Houston, but this option, though obvious to them, was never given any serious thought. They were determined to die in the Alamo at the threshold of Texas. The thirteen days that the defenders delayed the Mexican Army's advance was of incalculable value to Sam Houston and to the settlers between the Guadalupe and Brazos Rivers. It allowed

Houston to rally fighters to the cause and the settlers to escape eastward. It should be noted that the Alamo defenders were mostly Anglo but included a number of Hispanics. The defenders never received confirmation that independence had officially been declared on March 2. They died for a republic whose existence they would never know.

VI. GOLIAD

THE MOST TERRIBLE ATROCITY OF THE REVOLUTION WAS the massacre at Goliad, which occurred two weeks after the fall of the Alamo. Much pity and contempt for James Fannin is deserved for his foolhardy plan to invade Mexico with far too few people and too little support. However, just after the Texans' successful capture of San Antonio in the Battle of Béxar, the General Council at San Felipe was the one that gave Fannin a semblance of authority for an invasion via Matamoros. The Council certainly has blood on its hands for this ill-fated mission, as does Fannin.

Colonel Fannin had a little West Point training and is, perhaps, an example of "a little learning is a dangerous thing." His plan was to "carry the war into Mexico to keep it out of Texas." Fannin, John Grant, and Frank Johnson—who each had their own ideas of attacking Mexico—rushed their schemes for a descent upon Matamoros while the Alamo remained isolated. General Houston, who had been named Commander-in-Chief the previous November, traveled to these factions to attempt to organize them. Neither Grant, nor Johnson, nor Fannin would act with the others, nor with Houston, having *all* been given directions from the General Council. Houston's plans for an organized defense of

Texas were greatly frustrated by the failure of these men to acknowledge his authority while they functioned independently and in such a futile manner.

Meanwhile, Santa Anna had been advised of the Texans' invasion plans and sent General José Urrea with fifteen hundred men to Matamoros and then north into Texas—a force far superior to the combined forces of the fractured Texans. None of the Texan leaders even made it to Matamoros. On February 27, General Urrea's division attacked Johnson's small command which was aimlessly scouting the country at San Patricio and killed all but Johnson and four others who escaped. Four days later, on March 2, the very day the convention at Washington-on-the-Brazos declared independence, Grant's command was attacked by Urrea at Agua Dulce, and all but one were killed or captured (see Figure 2 for a map of locations, troop movements, and battles).

Fannin would soon be at the mercy of Urrea's army. While en route to Matamoros, he had occupied the mission/fortress Presidio La Bahía in Goliad and renamed it Fort Defiance. From there he had started many plans of action and abandoned all of them, including a relief effort directed towards the Alamo which never made it beyond sight of the Presidio. When word came to him on March 10 that the citizens of Refugio (pronounced Ree-FYUR-ee-oh) had been attacked, Fannin ordered Amon King to that town with twenty-eight men and wagons to aid in evacuating the remaining families, but within forty-eight hours those men were surrounded by Urrea's army. Fannin then ordered Lieutenant Colonel William Ward with one hundred fifty volunteers to aid King. All of the men dispatched in both campaigns were killed except for approximately one hundred of Ward's men who escaped to Victoria, only to be captured on March 22 and sent back to Goliad to meet their fate with Colonel Fannin.

Fannin's Folly

Fannin had previously been ordered by Houston to retreat to Victoria following news of the fall of the Alamo. He either ignored the order or circumstances prevented him from executing it. He did finally attempt a retreat from Goliad at the last moment and succeeded only in getting some miles when his detachment halted in an open prairie against all military wisdom. They were soon surrounded and attacked from all sides in what became known as the Battle of Coleto. The Texans defended themselves bravely but could not withstand the larger force surrounding them. The battle started at 3:00 P.M. on March 19 and lasted until sundown.

After dark the Texans strengthened their defenses by moving dead animals and bodies to create a makeshift barrier, but the lack of food and water, combined with exhaustion from the day's labor, rendered their efforts ineffective. Survivors described that night as one of great horror. Dawn brought the sight of one hundred Mexican reinforcements and three cannons joining the enemy force. With a little over two hundred effective fighting men, the Texans were in extreme peril. Given the circumstances, it was generally agreed among them that if an honorable capitulation could be obtained they would lay down their arms and surrender as prisoners of war. A white flag was raised, and the surrender was made.

Under the terms of the March 20 negotiated surrender, Fannin was to be treated with all consideration possible, and the whole detachment was to be treated as prisoners of war.

The prisoners were marched back to Goliad and would be joined in the coming days by one hundred sixty additional prisoners of war. General Urrea wished to treat the prisoners humanely and stated later in his *Diario* that he gave Fannin assurances that he would use his influence with the government to spare their lives; he did so accordingly in a letter to Santa Anna. Urrea also wrote to Lieutenant Colonel José Nicolás de la Portilla to that effect on March 26. He was the Mexican Commandant at Goliad following the Texan abandonment of the fort. But Urrea knew the Supreme Government had issued a decree that all foreigners taken in arms should be executed as pirates and traitors.

Santa Anna was apprised of the capture of Fannin and his troops, and he quickly dispatched an order to Portilla commanding him to immediately execute the prisoners and expressing his surprise that he had not already done so. That message was received by Portilla on the same day as Urrea's letter. Thus, despite the negotiated surrender, the entire command was marched out in several directions at dawn on Palm Sunday, March 27, and shot to death. Santa Anna, while in captivity after the war, refused to take responsibility for the action and blamed Commandant Portilla.

Colonel Fannin was reserved and met his fate with calmness. Given a wound he had received during the Battle of Coleto, he was not required to march but was executed inside the Presidio. He traded his watch to the officer in charge of the execution in exchange for a promise to not be shot in the head and for a decent burial. The watch was accepted; he, however, was shot in the head, his body stripped, and thrown onto the pile.

About twenty Texans who were physicians or otherwise thought to have some use were spared, and about another thirty Texans escaped. Three hundred and sixty-four prisoners of war, most of whom were under the protection of the surrender agreement, were murdered and left unburied. Ironically Presidio La Bahía was a military fort designed to be defended, and it never was. The Alamo was not a military fort, and yet the Texans made every effort to defend it.

It should be noted that General Urrea, in recommending that the prisoners be shown mercy, was reprimanded by Santa Anna for his position. In his *Diario,* Urrea repeatedly mentions that the Texans fought with great bravery. He says of Fannin and his men,

> Had I been in a position to do so, I would have at least guaranteed them their life. Fannin was a gentleman, a man of courage, a quality that makes us soldiers esteem each other mutually. His manners captivated my affection, and if it had been in my hand to save him, together with his companions, I would have gladly done so.

Commandant Portilla hesitated carrying out Santa Anna's orders and later expressed his horror and disgust at having to execute this horrible task. Even so, they both capitulated to the command of Santa Anna and share in the odium of this horrible deed.

VII. THE RUNAWAY SCRAPE

News of the fall and massacre at the Alamo traveled fast and settlers began a hurried and disorganized retreat towards Louisiana to outrun the advancing Mexican Army which was also moving east in a clean-up operation. An eyewitness in Gonzales on the evening of March 8 told of terror inspired by rumors arriving from the Alamo. The night was filled with the screams of women and children whose husbands and fathers had been killed in that disaster. The families of thirty-two men had seen their husbands, fathers, and brothers depart for the Alamo less than two weeks before, never to return.

General Houston arrived at Gonzales from Washington-on-the-Brazos on March 11, finding 374 men with less than two day's provisions, half-clothed, many without weapons or ammunition, and disorganized. Only a few had any knowledge of military tactics or discipline. Every available wagon but one was employed to move women and children. The sole other wagon was devoted to the removal of the munitions of war, and it was not overloaded. Alamo widow Susanna Dickinson arrived at Gonzales on March 13 along with her fellow survivor Joe and confirmed the news as eyewitnesses to the disaster, adding many terrible details. With no force available to repel the enemy, Houston began his retreat that same day, having thrown the only two cannons he had into the Guadalupe River since he had no way of transporting them. He and his militia departed Gonzales just before midnight after burning the town to the ground so as not to have it fall into enemy hands.

Texan reinforcements came up continually to join the retreat eastward, but many left upon hearing the news coming from the Alamo. When the retreat reached the Colorado River, Houston reported his strength at six hundred men but no artillery. The militia halted at the Colorado until all non-combatants had crossed, and then descended the east bank of the river to a place near the town of Columbus and camped for a week. As reinforcements arrived, the militia quickly swelled to between twelve hundred and fourteen hundred men. This number would rise and fall rapidly as men came and went freely. It was here on the Colorado that they learned about Fannin's fall at Goliad.

A Mexican Army division under the command of General Joaquin Ramírez y Sesma, numbering between six hundred and eight hundred soldiers came into view and camped on the opposite bank of the Colorado a few miles upstream. Houston could have engaged the enemy with superior numbers but chose not to risk a battle and was criticized severely. In comments to Captain R. L. Calder of the volunteer militia, Houston confided,

> To be sure, we could have whipped the Mexicans back at the Colorado; but we can't fight battles without having men killed and wounded. But we actually have

> not the means of conveying as much ammunition and baggage as we need, much less the means of conveying wounded men after an action; besides, a defeat to the enemy at the Colorado would inevitably have concentrated other divisions of the Mexican army against us.

Indeed, Houston knew the Mexican Army was moving by division, each of which was as large or larger than his entire militia, and enemy reinforcements could arrive quickly in an engagement. The Texas militia was comprised solely of light infantry, and it would be fighting against cavalry and artillery. Houston, therefore, felt it wise to deal with the troops' rebellious attitude rather than acquiesce to their wishes and lose the war instantly. History suggests that Houston's assessment was right. Retreat and silence were his chosen course of action, and he took no one into his own counsel. Houston stood alone against the pressure of his government and his militia.

The Texan militia, as well as the western population of Texas, fell back east to the Brazos River, the militia arriving at San Felipe de Austin on March 26 with a force that had been reduced by half due to mutiny. At times General Houston would attempt to hide the mutinies by issuing orders to the departing men to go wherever they were already headed in an effort to make it look like he was in control. Those orders often took the form of, "Fall back and cover the rear." It can be said that the militia at this point was perhaps more of a disorganized armed mob. Once, Houston even resorted to trickery to hold his militia together. As he was sending a courier to Secretary of War Thomas J. Rusk, he called the courier back to him and wrote on the outside of the dispatch that the Texas militia would soon total fifteen hundred men before sending the courier on his way. This was an intentional fabrication that Houston knew would get disseminated among the troops and serve to reduce their mutinous attitude. And it did seem to have that effect for a time. Houston took no one into his confidence regarding his plan, and at times it seemed there would be open mutiny as he was often misunderstood as not having any plan other than retreat.

Heavy rains in March and April made it difficult for both armies to move. In his effort to effect a crossing of the Brazos, Houston moved north along the west bank of the river, while the Mexican army moved south to Fort Bend, also looking to cross.

One of the many graphic pictures of the Runaway Scrape, as this hurried, disorganized, and anxious retreat between the fall of the Alamo and the victory at San Jacinto became known, is related by Rosa Kleberg, telling of the flight of all Texas. (Mrs. Kleberg would have eight children, one of whom, Robert, would marry Alice Gertrudis King and assume management of the King Ranch.) At the time, Mrs. Kleberg was twenty-two years old and lived in Cat Spring, Texas. Her husband and brothers had joined the militia, while the women in the family, along with the father, were migrating towards the east and the safety of Louisiana. Rosa spoke no English, having immigrated to Texas from Westphalia less than two years earlier. In her own words, translated from German:

Figure 1: Texas in 1835. Land Grants and Colonies.

Figure 2:
Major military campaigns of
the 1836 Texas Revolution

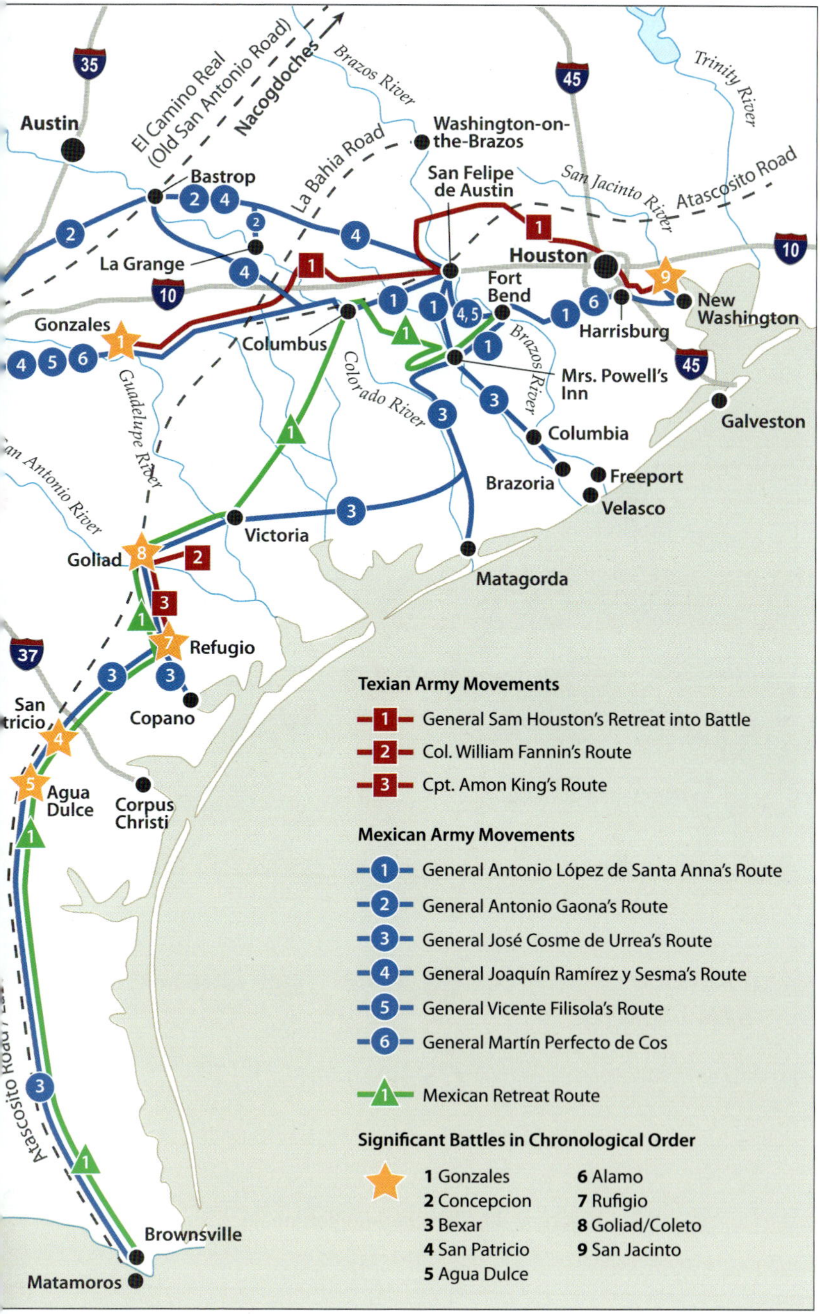
Austin
El Camino Real
(Old San Antonio Road)
Nacogdoches
Brazos River
Washington-on-
the-Brazos
Trinity River
Bastrop
La Bahia Road
San Felipe
de Austin
San Jacinto River
Atascosito Road
La Grange
Houston
Fort
Bend
Harrisburg
New
Washington
Gonzales
Columbus
Colorado River
Brazos River
Mrs. Powell's
Inn
Galveston
Guadelupe River
an Antonio River
Columbia
Brazoria
Freeport
Velasco
Victoria
Goliad
Matagorda
Refugio
San
tricio
Copano
Agua
Dulce
Corpus
Christi
Atascosito Road
Brownsville
Matamoros
Texian Army Movements
1 General Sam Houston's Retreat into Battle
2 Col. William Fannin's Route
3 Cpt. Amon King's Route
Mexican Army Movements
1 General Antonio López de Santa Anna's Route
2 General Antonio Gaona's Route
3 General José Cosme de Urrea's Route
4 General Joaquín Ramírez y Sesma's Route
5 General Vicente Filisola's Route
6 General Martín Perfecto de Cos
1 Mexican Retreat Route
Significant Battles in Chronological Order
1 Gonzales
2 Concepcion
3 Bexar
4 San Patricio
5 Agua Dulce
6 Alamo
7 Rufigio
8 Goliad/Coleto
9 San Jacinto

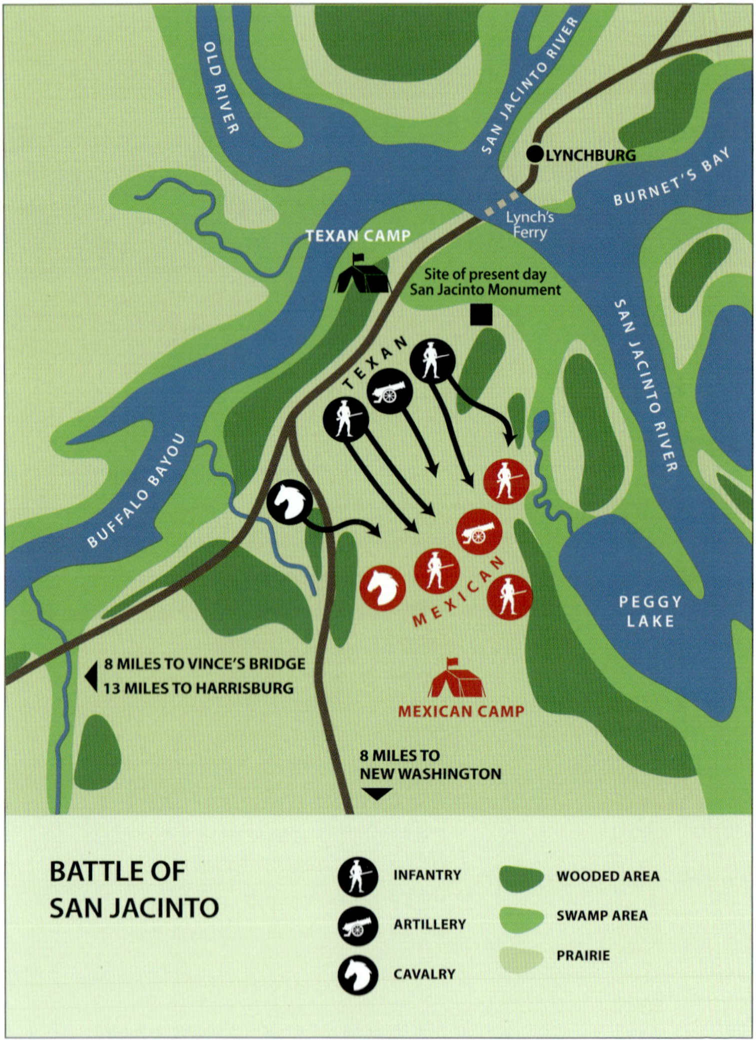

Figure 3: The San Jacinto battlefield

Figure 4: Map of the Republic of Texas

Figure 5: Independence Hall at Washington, Texas, aka Washington-on-the-Brazos, as it appeared in 1893

Figure 6: The First Capitol Building of Texas in Columbia, Texas, circa 1897

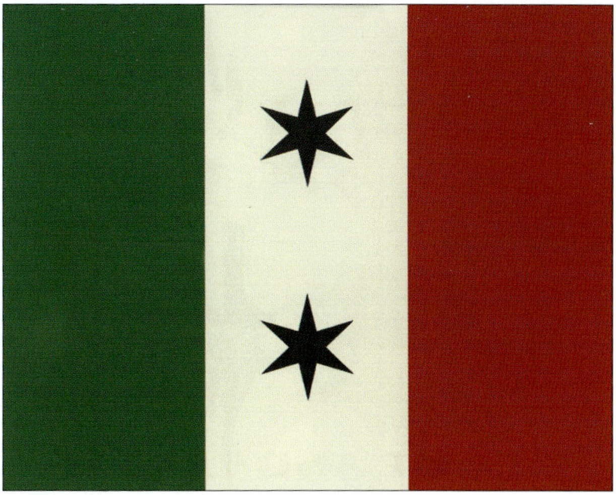

Figure 7: Two-Star Tricolor Flag. This is one of three flags known to have flown over the Alamo during the siege of 1836. It is a modification of the Mexican flag with the two stars representing the proposed separation of the State of Coahuila y Texas into two states. It was a reminder to Mexico that the settlers were denied separate statehood while trying to stay loyal to the Mexican nation.

Figure 8: 1824 Tricolor Flag. The Texans replaced the eagle on the Mexican flag with the numbers 1824, a reference to the year of the Mexican Federal Constitution which guaranteed freedoms to the settlers. As in the case of the Two-Star Tricolor Flag, it was a sharp rebuke to the Mexican nation that they had been denied their rights as Mexican citizens under the nullified Constitution of 1824.

Figure 9: Come and Take It Flag. The flag of the Gonzales Brigade who dared the Mexican army to try to confiscate their cannon, which was given to them four years before by the Mexican Government for defense against the Indians.

Figure 10: National Standard Flag of the Republic of Texas. This was the first official flag of the Republic of Texas. Although it had been replaced before annexation, it fits Noah Smithwick's description of the flag lowered by Republic President Anson Jones February 19, 1846, on the steps of the old capitol building as he ceded power to the Governor of Texas.

> Most of the families travelled separately until they reached the Brazos, where all were compelled to halt for a crossing. I helped drive the cattle and carried my infant daughter in the saddle before me. When the families and their horses and cattle reached the crossing, the noise was terrible. There was only one small ferry boat, which would carry one vehicle at a time. Deaf Smith's Mexican wife was in a cart with two wooden wheels made from an entire cross-section of a large tree, with her two pairs of twins, but had no team to pull her cart. My brother carried her for a distance with his yoke of oxen. The next day after we crossed over the Brazos we camped near Clear Creek, where Louis V. Roeder, my brother's child, was born in a corn crib.

When Rosa Kleberg would return to her homestead following the Texas victory at San Jacinto, she would find her house and most of her remaining worldly possessions burned by the Mexican army. She would have to start over with less than she had when she arrived in Texas.

Meanwhile, the ad interim government which had organized at Washington-on-the-Brazos in March was retreating east, hurried by reports that General Sesma's army was approaching. President ad interim David Burnet hurriedly sent messages to General Houston to stop his retreat and fight, even as he continued his own retreat to Galveston. Burnet's flight would take him through the settlements of Harrisburg and the optimistically named New Washington on the way to Galveston.

Santa Anna arrived at Harrisburg just after Burnet's departure and burned the town to the ground. The dictator then sent his trusted aide-de-camp Juan Almonte in pursuit of the government, and this detachment reached New Washington just as Burnet and his officials were pulling away from a pier in a rowboat. The rowboat was fired upon but General Almonte ordered the firing to stop when he saw a woman on board, Burnet's wife. But for her, they would have certainly all been killed.

J. H. Kuykendall in his recollections of the campaign recounts that Houston was well aware of the mutinous feelings of his militia which was angry that the general would not stand and fight. Kuykendall remembers the general addressing his group in a driving rain:

> My friends, I am told that evil disposed persons have told you that I am going to march you to the Redlands [meaning to Louisiana, safety, and avoidance of a fight]. This is false. I am going to march you into the Brazos bottom near Groce's [Jared Groce's plantation was south of what is now Hempstead, Texas, on the east bank of the Brazos River; part of Groce's land grant is currently owned by the author's family], to a position where you can whip the enemy ten to one.

Indeed the militia did march to Groce's Retreat (the name Jared Groce gave to his plantation) and camped there for twelve or thirteen days. Houston used these days to try to train and discipline the troops, but the volunteers did not take well to discipline.

While here, the general received a bit of welcome news. Santa Anna, on his way east towards the Brazos River, had made an unwelcomed stop at Mrs. Elizabeth Powell's inn and inadvertently divulged some useful information.

Mrs. Powell, a widow, had not participated in the Runaway Scrape and had chosen to shelter in place at her house, a common dog-run style wooden structure where she rented rooms to travelers. It was located at a well-traveled crossroad over the San Bernard River. During Santa Anna's stay he held a council of war and determined that he would personally lead a column of soldiers in the direction of Harrisburg. Upon the departure of the Mexican army and its leader, Mrs. Powell's house and all of her outbuildings would be burned to the ground by the intruders.

Unknown to Santa Anna, Mrs. Powell's teenage son spoke Spanish and had overheard his plan. This intelligence was quickly relayed to Sam Houston by horse and rider. Based in part on this information, Houston and his militia crossed to the east bank of the Brazos River on April 12–14 using the steam tugboat *Yellowstone* there at Groce's Retreat in anticipation of continuing eastward. It was here that the militia joyfully received the Twin Sisters—two field artillery pieces gifted to the Texas cause by the citizens of Cincinnati, Ohio.

Still there was open talk in the ranks about replacing Houston with a more aggressive leader should Houston continue to avoid battle. And the size of the militia changed daily as volunteers arrived and others mutinied.

Seemingly all of Texas was now east of the Brazos River. Divisions of the Mexican Army were sweeping through the country north as far as the San Antonio-Nacogdoches Road and south along the coast. Meanwhile His Excellency Santa Anna, with what he called the flower of the Army, hurried along in advance and crossed the Brazos at Fort Bend to push towards the fleeing ad interim government at Harrisburg (located in what is now southeast Houston near Loop 610 and Highway 225). He would divert north to San Jacinto only after capturing Harrisburg.

It was there at Harrisburg that the *Telegraph and Texas Register*—a newspaper which had published the Texas Declaration of Independence—was also captured, along with three workers who divulged the whereabouts and strength of the Texas militia. Santa Anna also learned from them that the Texas Government officials had left in the direction of Galveston that morning.

The Texas militia began its journey east from Groce's Retreat on the evening of April 14. They would soon learn that Santa Anna had made his crossing over the Brazos at Fort Bend as he headed for Harrisburg. Shortly thereafter, Houston's militia reached Charles Donoho's plantation (four miles southeast of Hempstead) where it reunited with various detachments which had been ordered back by Houston to consolidate his forces.

Fifteen miles ahead, at the site of what is now New Kentucky Park in far northwest Houston, lay an impending fork in the road—a physical and mental crossroad that would define a nation and a destiny. The left fork directed the militia through Nacogdoches to Louisiana and safety; the right fork transported them to Harrisburg and battle. Many expected a scene at the fork, and it was generally agreed among the rank-and-file that if the Commander-in-Chief did not order or permit the militia to take the right fork, he was to be disposed of his command then and there. It is not known if Houston ordered the men to take the right fork or if that decision was made by the men. What we do know is that on April 16, the militia took the right fork towards battle, and there was no dissent from anyone, including General Houston.

So, as the opposing sides flung themselves towards a collision at San Jacinto, we find an overconfident Santa Anna with his well-supplied army and the grim and silent Sam Houston with his unhappy, disorganized hundreds crossing the muddy prairies between the Brazos and San Jacinto rivers. All the while, thousands of fleeing families hurried their weary way across the Trinity River towards the safety of Louisiana, their towns and livelihoods burned behind them—either by the settlers themselves so as not to fall into enemy hands, or by the scorched-earth campaign of the Mexican Army. Without any doubt, the volunteer militia would have come into regular contact with the fleeing families who filled every road going east by the thousands. Together they moved over swollen rivers and muddy paths exposed to cold spring northers and rain. The scene was distressing and definitely served to focus the nerves of the volunteer militia headed into certain battle.

VIII. SAN JACINTO

Following his victory at the Alamo, Santa Anna had planned a victorious return to Mexico, leaving the mop-up operation in the hands of his capable second in command, General Vicente Filísola. Santa Anna had received word that his vice president, who was in charge of the government in his absence, had passed away, and he became anxious about his power base back home. But the only way he could effect a quick return to Mexico City was by sea, and the Texas Navy had rendered his vessel incapacitated. In light of the circumstances, he was dissuaded to return by General Almonte and other officers. He made the decision to stay and conduct the remainder of the war personally.

Santa Anna did not seem to contemplate any serious opposition. He had come to Texas with seventy-five hundred soldiers but had divided his army into divisions scattered from the coast to Béxar.

General Sesma with one thousand of those soldiers was to be the spearhead of the operation, driving up the center of populated Texas from west to east, chasing Sam Houston in his retreat from the Brazos. The spring floods, however, prevented him from close pursuit, and Sesma ended up at Fort Bend. General Antonio Gaona, with 750 men, was deployed along the left flank and heading towards Nacogdoches, but he was diverted and went no further north than Bastrop, ending up near La Grange. General Urrea was marching along the coast from Goliad with fifteen hundred men on the right flank. General Filísola was nearby with two thousand soldiers, coming down the Brazos from San Felipe seeking a crossing. Santa Anna with his six or seven hundred soldiers was in pursuit of the fledgling Texas Government at Harrisburg, arriving there the night of April 15. And General Cós with five hundred was trying to keep up with Santa Anna's cavalry but lagging behind. These divisions along with stationary detachments at Goliad, Béxar, Copano, and Matagorda represented the entire Mexican force in Texas. (For a reference map of Texan and Mexican troop movements, see Figure 2.)

Santa Anna had split his army into multiple divisions in an effort to encircle and trap the Texan militia. He sent word to General Houston that as soon as he cleaned out the "land thieves" (meaning the government officials and probably the retreating settlers east of the Trinity), he would pay his respects to Houston. Meanwhile Houston received the following message from his government:

> Executive Department,
> Harrisburg, April 1836
> To Gen. Sam Houston.
>
> Sir: The enemy are laughing you to scorn. You must fight them. You must retreat no further. The country

> expects you to fight. The salvation of your country depends on you doing so.
>
> —DAVID G. BURNET

Ad interim President Burnet disliked Sam Houston with a passion, and Burnet went to his grave thinking him a coward. Sam Houston, for his part, thought the president's skills were on par with a common clerk and had nicknamed him *Wetumpka*—Cherokee for "hog thief"—which of course infuriated the president. Burnet and others charged that General Houston never intended to fight, that he intended to retreat to the Louisiana border in hopes of getting help from General Edmund Gaines of the United States Army who was camped there, or worse yet, that he sought refuge with the American Army. While it is evident that Houston hoped for help from Gaines—help which never came—he wrote a letter on March 19 to Colonel Henry Rouget of the Committee of Safety at Nacogdoches deploring the fact that no help had come from the U.S. Army and announcing that he was now about to cross the bayou for the purpose of attacking Santa Anna's army. Here are excerpts from that letter:

> This morning we are in preparation to meet Santa Anna. It is the only chance of saving Texas ... It is wisdom growing out of necessity to meet and fight the enemy now. Every consideration enforces it. No previous occasion would justify it. The troops are in fine spirits, and now is the time for action.

General Houston had learned definitively on March 18, the day before he wrote this letter, that the Mexican advance force had passed Harrisburg and that Santa Anna was with it. Erastus "Deaf" Smith, a nearly-deaf spy who is said to have had other senses in extraordinary measure, had captured a Mexican express courier (near what is now the corner of Bellaire Boulevard and Rice Avenue in Houston) who had in his possession a pair of deerskin saddlebags full of documents intended for Santa Anna. The saddlebags bore the name of William Travis—a trophy from the Alamo. Its contents detailed the strength, plans, and movements of the enemy. General Houston now knew where Santa Anna was, where he was heading, and the strength of his force.

Trapped

Armed with this information, Houston and his militia of settlers/adventurers pushed down to the confluence of Buffalo Bayou and the San Jacinto River, crossing Buffalo Bayou just below the mouth of Sims Bayou (near the intersection of modern-day Loop 610 and Highway 225 in southeast Houston), by way of "Vince's Bridge," completing their march well after midnight in the early morning hours of April 20. The general was rushing to insert his militia into the path of Santa Anna. Before crossing the bayou, according to Dr. N. D. Labadie who was a volunteer in the militia, Houston made an animated speech, towards the conclusion of which he said, "The army will cross, and we will meet the enemy. Some of us may be killed and will be killed; but soldiers, remember the Alamo, the Alamo! The Alamo!" In response, one solder was reported to have said, "[And] Damn few will be taken prisoner!" They were, in fact, intent on achieving liberty or dying for the cause—a cause which they considered greater than themselves in that fateful year of 1836, and which remains so today among those who value Freedom.

James W. Winters, another volunteer, wrote that it was absolutely Houston's intent to head off the Mexican army at Lynch's Ferry (located at the confluence of the San Jacinto River and Buffalo Bayou), and he was in such a hurry that they did not take time to prepare or eat meals.

In the remaining hours before dawn the militia—having reached their intended destination—camped in some woods on what would become the San Jacinto Battleground, near where the Battleship *Texas* was docked in more recent times. This site was chosen to prevent Santa Anna from crossing the San Jacinto River at Lynch's Ferry. In front of the Texans and extending to the right was an open prairie about two miles wide, bounded on the south by a marsh; to their left was the San Jacinto River; and at their backs was Buffalo Bayou. Both waterways were swollen by the heavy spring rains (see Figure 3 for the layout of the battleground).

Santa Anna in his *Manifesto* published in 1837 claims to have been "in a position to choose the location for battle; and I shut up the enemy in the low marshy angle of the country where his retreat was cut off by Buffalo Bayou and the San Jacinto [River]." That claim does not seem to fit the facts, given that the Texans arrived first, although perhaps the Mexican general thought he had the Texas militia cornered, which would not have been an exaggeration. General Houston was indeed trapped by Buffalo Bayou and the San Jacinto River, but that is where he had placed himself and his militia intentionally. The only way out for the Texas militia was through the Mexican army.

After daylight that same morning, April 20, Santa Anna's army came into sight of the Texas militia. Into this prairie the Mexicans soon flooded from the south—the direction of New Washington, which they had just burned—and formed their camp near the southern edge, about a mile away. Early in the afternoon, Santa Anna advanced their one cannon under cover of the cavalry and fired upon the Texans, but this being immediately returned from the Twin Sisters, the cannon was hastily withdrawn to the protection of a cluster of trees from which it continued to be fired at intervals for the rest of the afternoon. Colonel Sidney Sherman, according to his own account, asked for and was granted permission to advance with mounted volunteers and attempt to capture the cannon. This succeeded in little more than causing a lively skirmish with the Mexican cavalry and created a good deal of excitement in the Texan camp. Two Texans were wounded, one of whom died afterwards. Little else of consequence happened that day, although it appears that Houston wavered in his determination to confront this disciplined enemy in battle, still hoping for reinforcements to arrive soon. His troops, on the other hand, were anxious for a fight. Across the battlefield Santa Anna was content to wait, knowing that his reinforcements would arrive in the morning.

Eighteen Minutes that Shook the World

Reinforcements did indeed come, but not for the Texans. On April 21, the high holy day of Texas independence, General Cós caught up to and joined Santa Anna's force, swelling the number under Santa Anna's command to between eleven and twelve hundred men (Texan accounts put the number as high as fifteen hundred). Sam Houston, with his 783 men, held a council of war with his officers in which it was debated whether they should attack the enemy or wait for the enemy to attack them. It was well known that the Mexican Army was composed of veteran soldiers and that very few Texans had ever seen battle other than Indian warfare.

The war council adjourned, and still Houston kept his silence, not expressing his designs to anyone, furthering criticism that he did not have a plan or did not intend to fight. But Houston now had his opportunity at somewhat reasonable odds, and the Mexican dictator was in command of the army in front of him. He walked through the camp, preferring to get the opinions of the men themselves as to their will to fight—they had, after all, marched days through mud and water with little food or rest. He concluded by saying, "Fellow soldiers, there is the enemy before you; do you wish to fight?" "We do!" was the universal response. "Well then, remember it is for liberty, or death!—Remember the Alamo! Remember Goliad!"

General Cós's forces, which had joined Santa Anna that morning, were exhausted from their long forced march, and Santa Anna, seeing that apparently no offensive was forthcoming from the Texans that day, instructed the army to stack their arms and rest, certain that the battle would be engaged the next day. That decision proved to be a costly mistake for his soldiers and his empire.

At 3:30 that afternoon, Houston summoned Colonel John Wharton and ordered him to form the Texan militia for an immediate offensive. According to Dr. Labadie, his exact words to Wharton were, "Fight and be damned." The excitement was intense, and if the grim old Cherokee chief had intended to work his men up to the point of frenzy for a fight, he had managed it well in the end.

In his battle report to President David Burnet, dated April 25, 1836, Sam Houston writes:

> I have the honor to inform you, that on the evening of the 18th, after a forced march of fifty-five miles [the distance from Groce's Retreat], which was effected in two and a half days, the army arrived opposite Harrisburg. That evening a courier of the enemy was taken, from whom I learned that General Santa Anna, with one division of his choice troops, had marched in the direction of Lynch's Ferry, on the San Jacinto—burning Harrisburg as he passed down . . .
>
> On the morning of the 19th, [we] left the baggage, the sick and a sufficient camp guard in the rear

[numbering between one hundred fifty and two hundred according to Moseley Baker's account] ... At daylight [on the 20th] ... our scouts encountered those of the enemy, and we received information that Santa Anna was at New Washington and would that day take up the line of march for Anahuac crossing at Lynch's Ferry. The Texian army halted within a half mile of the Ferry in some timber ... when the army of Santa Anna was discovered to be approaching in battle array.

About nine o'clock in the morning of the 21st, the enemy were reinforced with 500 choice troops under the command of General Cós, increasing their force to upwards of 1500 men, whilst our aggregate force for the field numbered 783. At half past three o'clock in the evening, I ordered the officers of the Texian army to parade their respective commands, having in the meantime ordered the bridge ["Vince's Bridge"] on the only road communicating with the Brazos, distant eight miles from our encampment, to be destroyed, thus cutting off all possibility of escape. Our troops ... were anxious for the contest. Their conscious disparity in numbers seemed only to increase their enthusiasm and confidence and heighten their anxiety for the conflict. The first regiment, commanded by Colonel Burleson, was assigned to the center. The second regiment, under the command of Colonel Sherman, formed the left wing of the army. The artillery under the special command of Colonel George W. Hockley, was placed on the right of the first regiment; and four

> companies of infantry under the command of Lieut.-Col. Henry Millard, sustained the artillery upon the right. Our cavalry, sixty-one in number, commanded by Colonel Mirabeau B. Lamar, placed on our extreme right, completed our line [see Figure 3]. Our cavalry was first dispatched to the front of the enemy's left. Every evolution was performed with alacrity, the whole advancing rapidly through an open prairie, without any protection whatever for our men.

Additionally, Colonel Juan Seguin, who had previously provided help rallying the Mexican population in and around San Antonio de Béxar to the patriots' cause, had volunteered his services, and had been appointed captain in the army. Seguin commanded his company of Mexican volunteers as the rear guard of the operation beginning on April 19. Houston continued:

> Colonel Sherman, with his regiment, having commenced the action upon our left wing, the whole line at the center and on the right, advancing in double-quick time, rung the war cry, "Remember the Alamo," received the enemy's fire and advanced within point blank shot before a piece was discharged from our lines. Our line advanced without a halt, until they were in possession of the woodland and the breastwork . . . The conflict lasted about eighteen minutes from the time of close action until we were in possession of the enemy's encampment . . . Many of the troops encountered hand to hand [combat], and not having the advantage

of bayonets on our side, our riflemen used pieces [their rifles] as war clubs, breaking many of them off at the breech. The rout commenced at half past four, and the pursuit [of the scattering Mexican army] by the main army continued until twilight. In the battle our loss was two killed and twenty-three wounded, six of them mortally. The enemy's loss was 630 killed. Wounded: 208. Prisoners: 730. General Santa Anna was not taken until the 22nd, and General Cós on yesterday, very few having escaped.

For several days previous to the action our troops were engaged in forced marches, exposed to excessive rains, and the additional inconvenience of extremely bad roads, badly supplied with rations and clothing; yet, amid every difficulty, they bore up with cheerfulness and fortitude . . .

Colonel Thos. J. Rusk, Secretary of War, was on the field . . . on the left wing, where Colonel Sherman's command first encountered and drove the enemy . . . Nor should we withhold the tribute of our grateful thanks, from that Being who rules the destinies of nations, and has in the time of greatest need enabled us to arrest a powerful invader, whilst devastating our Country.

I have the honor to be with high consideration, your obedient servant,

—SAM HOUSTON, *Commander in Chief*

At the onset of the battle, the Mexican camp was in complete disarray, many having been awakened from sleep. No significant defense was organized, although Generals Almonte and Castrillón attempted to rally the troops but were unable to stop the exodus of soldiers fleeing for their lives. In his journal Colonel Pedro Delgado of Santa Anna's staff says of the battle,

> I saw our men flying in small groups, terrified, and sheltering themselves behind large trees . . . They were a bewildered and panic-stricken herd . . . I saw His Excellency lying down to avoid grape shots . . . Then I saw His Excellency running about in the utmost excitement, wringing his hands and unable to give an order.

Mexican soldiers were heard crying, "Me no Alamo! Me no Goliad!" to no avail. Though the battle lasted only eighteen minutes, the revenge killing went on until dark. Sam Houston, appalled at the bloodlust, repeatedly ordered it to stop, but he was ignored. He was reported to have finally said in frustration, "Gentlemen! Gentlemen! I applaud your bravery but damn your manners."

During the rout General Castrillón was offered a horse by his men to escape on, but he refused, stating that he had never turned his back in battle and would die like a soldier. Indeed he did, and in his belongings was found David Crockett's journal.

Texan fighter James W. Winters made some interesting observations about the campaign, including that after they departed Harrisburg for San Jacinto, they had no more wagons and packed everything on their backs.

Further, the Mexican breastworks were composed of baggage, saddle bags, and brush piled about four or five feet high with a gap in the middle through which they fired the cannon. He also noted that General Houston had two horses killed from under him and was on his third before he passed the Mexican breastworks. In Winter's own words, "We ran and fought fully two miles."

The greatest slaughter in the battle occurred between the breastworks and the lake behind the Mexican camp. Here the enemy soldiers and horses killed were so numerous that they formed a bridge across the bayou. Many fled into the marshes and bayous where they drowned. A few Texan soldiers pursued the fleeing Mexicans as far as "Vince's Bridge" eight miles away. The Mexicans, finding the bridge burned, tried to cross but their horses bogged. Only one escaped—all others were shot.

Victory

By sundown the destruction of the Mexican army under Santa Anna's direct command was complete. One million square miles of river, forest, mountain, and plain were lost to the dictator and his nation. Texas, at that time, reached into Wyoming as far north as the 42nd parallel which is also the northern boundary of present-day California, and included parts of five additional current states (see Figure 4).

Well-regarded historians have called the Battle of San Jacinto one of the most decisive battles in world history, along with the likes of Napoleon's victory at Waterloo.

San Jacinto decided the fate not only of the Texas colonies but opened the door for the United States to move west to the Pacific and north to Oregon.

In the immediate aftermath of the battle Sam Houston, having been injured by a musket shot to the foot, understood that other divisions of the Mexican Army were in the area and feared his Texans could still be overtaken. His fears were heightened when a large division of Mexican soldiers marched into view, and he shouted, "All is lost, all is lost; my God, all is lost!"

His concern was that the column of soldiers in front of him was Mexican General Filísola's army which had been in the area of Fort Bend and could now be heading into a renewed battle.

A volunteer by the name of Amasa Turner handed him a spy glass which Houston used to sight the approaching army.

"Is that Rusk?" Houston hopefully asked Turner.

In fact, he *was* looking at General Rusk marching Mexican General Almonte's famous Guerrero Division back as prisoners of war.

"Yes, certainly, that is Rusk with the prisoners," was Turner's reply, giving great relief to the general.

It was now about sunset, allowing Houston and his staff to depart the battlefield for the Texas camp.

On the following day, April 22, various parties were scouring the prairie on the lookout for Santa Anna and Cós. James Sylvester, a volunteer who had come to Texas to join the fight for independence, was near the bridge on

Vince's Bayou when he saw some deer that startled. He looked to discover what had caused them to stir and saw a Mexican soldier break towards the bayou. The man was captured and taken into camp. His identity was soon betrayed by subordinates who unwittingly addressed him as, "*El Presidente*," even though he had changed clothes and appeared quite common.

As he was being brought to Sam Houston, many Texans called for him to be shot or hanged, but Houston ordered those men to be taken away, and he received Santa Anna with dignity.

General Almonte translated the exchange between Santa Anna and Sam Houston. Santa Anna declared, "That man may consider himself born to no common destiny who has captured the Napoleon of the West; and it now remains for him to be generous to the vanquished."

Houston replied that he should have remembered the Alamo. Santa Anna claimed that he was only operating under orders of the government, to which Houston reminded him that, as dictator, he *was* the government; and reminded him of Goliad. The dictator refused to take responsibility.

Houston knew that Santa Anna was more valuable alive as an influence broker than he was dead as a soldier. In Santa Anna's own words, written in exile as an older man:

> Samuel Houston treated us in a way that could not have been hoped for. His humane and generous conduct

> . . . On recognizing me, he addressed me courteously, extending his hand. Despite his wounds, which he had received assaulting my camp, he interested himself with regard to my person, ordered my tent and cot to be prepared and placed near his. To those who begged reprisal, he said seriously, "There is no need of harboring resentment against the prisoners. They complied with the precepts of their government." I have always recalled with the sincerest gratitude how much I owed to this singular man in the saddest moments of my career.

Sam Houston did indeed treat Santa Anna with compassion, despite the Mexican general's cold-blooded murder of so many Texan prisoners of war following battles at the Alamo, Goliad, and elsewhere. But Houston was wise enough to recognize that Santa Anna could be a valuable tool in the recognition of Texas as a nation if kept alive. For his part, Santa Anna knew in a very real sense that he owed his life to Sam Houston.

A Free Nation

In Santa Anna's 1837 *Manifesto*, he refused to take personal blame for the action at San Jacinto. He blamed his officers, soldiers, lack of provision, fatigue, fate, and even "the ground we occupied." The latter claim is striking, given that previous paragraphs contained claims that he had chosen the location for battle, that he had foreseen everything, and conducted the operation well. He goes on to say, "None of these causes was the result of neglect on my part or of acts emanating from me." Antonio López de Santa Anna was a narcissist of the highest order.

The Battle of San Jacinto, coming after sixty days of intense excitement and following reverses of the terrible outcomes of the Alamo and Goliad, filled Texas with great rejoicing and its tidings were received throughout the United States with enthusiasm. Five days after the battle, General Houston wrote a message in lead pencil on a piece of paper no larger than a hand which was sent by messenger to U.S. General Edmund Gaines on the Sabine River. It was addressed to no one in particular and read:

> San Jacinto, April 26, 1836
>
> Tell our friends all the news, that we have beat the enemy, killed 630, taken 570 prisoners [this prisoner count is 200 less than his battle report dated one day prior, and he does not list the wounded]. General Santa Anna and Cós were taken, three generals slain. Vast amount of property taken and about 1500 standards of arms, many swords and one nine-pound cannon. Tell them to come on and let the people plant corn.
>
> —SAMUEL HOUSTON, *Commander in Chief*

Sam Houston had enjoyed a close relationship to Andrew Jackson—the American president having been a mentor to Houston for years. General Gaines directed Lieutenant Ethan Allen Hitchcock (named for his grandfather the American Revolutionary War hero) to deliver the dispatch to the president of the United States.

In his diary Hitchcock wrote,

> I never saw a man more delighted than President Jackson. He read the dispatch . . . exclaiming over and over as though talking to himself, "Yes, that is his writing. I know it well. That is Sam Houston's writing. There can be no doubt about what he says." Then the old man ordered a map and he and I spread it and tried to locate San Jacinto. He passed his finger excitedly over the map in search of the name, but it was not there. He would say, "It must be here . . . No, it is over there," as he ran his fingers back and forth over the map, but finally gave up the search. So great was his enthusiasm that I think he would have promoted me to a captain of dragoons on the spot had there been a vacancy.

Texas was its own free nation.

IX. THE REPUBLIC OF TEXAS

The Early Days

Though the independence of Texas had been declared at Washington-on-the-Brazos on March 2, 1836, it was not achieved until the close of April 21 at San Jacinto. The ad interim government which had retreated from Harrisburg to Galveston Island learned of the victory by messenger. President Burnet and Vice President de Zavala arrived at the battleground three days after the battle by steamer and began negotiations with Santa Anna. Houston sought medical attention in New Orleans, and at his request Secretary of War Thomas J. Rusk assumed command of the Texas Army.

Santa Anna had already agreed with Sam Houston to order the Mexican Army divisions to fall back to Béxar and Victoria, and ultimately to withdraw across the Rio Grande. There were still, after all, around five thousand Mexican Army regulars in Texas, including their most capable commander, General Filísola, who as Santa Anna's second in command was now in charge of the army. If the army would organize again for battle, the prospects of the new Republic could reverse in a moment. The Texas militia was still only a small fraction of the size of the Mexican force in Texas, and although it had a good supply of cattle and munitions, it lacked horses and flints. It was hardly an intimidating force. The sovereignty and stability of the Republic hung very much in the balance. General Filísola, however, obeyed Santa Anna's orders despite strong opposition from many officers, particularly General Urrea. As a result, the Texans' fears were not immediately realized, even though Texas would continue to deal with Mexican attempts to reclaim what they had lost during Texas' entire existence as a republic.

President Burnet negotiated two treaties with the dictator, one of which was public and the other secret. The open treaty provided that all hostility should cease, and that Santa Anna would not "exercise his influence to cause arms to be taken up against the people of Texas during the present war for independence."

In the secret treaty, in exchange for his immediate freedom, Santa Anna bound himself to

> so prepare things in the Cabinet of Mexico that a mission sent thither by the government of Texas may be well received and by means of negotiations all difference may be settled and independence acknowledged.

In other words, Santa Anna committed to engage politically on behalf of the new Republic to cause Mexico to officially recognize Texas as a sovereign nation.

These treaties were executed at the small Texas port town of Velasco, near what is now Freeport, on May 14. The Rio Grande would be the boundary, and Santa

Anna was to be returned to Mexico at once by way of Veracruz, embarking on the schooner *Invincible* at the mouth of the Brazos on June 3.

Just before sailing, a steamer arrived from New Orleans bearing two hundred fifty volunteers who had come to take part in the Revolution, albeit too late. These volunteers defied the government and took affairs into their own hands. They captured Santa Anna and took him hostage to a plantation above Columbia, Texas (known now as West Columbia, a few miles northwest of Angleton) until the following November.

President Burnet was powerless to resist the new recruits given that the Texas militia under Rusk had followed Filísola's forces as they retreated towards the Rio Grande in order to ensure their compliance. Santa Anna, of course, protested his detention in violation of the Velasco Treaty and would eventually disavow the treaty altogether, thus putting the safety and sovereignty of Texas at risk once again. It would be another twelve years before Mexican claims on Texas sovereignty would be fully and finally relinquished and incursions onto her soil abandoned.

Burnet called for elections in September, at which time the constitution adopted in March was ratified. Sam Houston was elected president by acclamation, and Mirabeau B. Lamar was elected vice president. The first Congress met pitifully on October 3 at Columbia, on the Brazos River, in a barn-like building in poverty (see Figure 6). Houston would serve as both the first and third president since the Constitution provided that the first president should serve for two years and not be eligible for immediate reelection.

The first Congress was charged with bringing order and system out of chaos and raising means where none existed. In the aftermath of the Revolution and the Runaway Scrape, Texas was disorganized, its people impoverished, and its Treasury exhausted. There was no law, no judiciary, the militia was starving, and most of the buildings had been destroyed in the Runaway Scrape. There were few roads in the traditional sense, as most were mere trails between destinations, often marked with notched trees and sometimes not easily followed. Though the nation and the freedoms for which they had fought existed in theory and on paper, Congress and the people had much work to do to reestablish order and raise means as a simple matter of survival.

Such were the conditions when the government of the Republic of Texas began on a tract of land that in later years became the great Columbia oil field.

Annexation and Slavery

Back in the United States, you would have thought that the Jackson administration's enthusiasm for acquiring Texas as a new American state would have led to an immediate annexation, which the new Republic had voted for almost unanimously in the recent September election. But Jackson was now in bad health and would soon vacate the presidency at the end of his second term. President-Elect Martin Van Buren was not enthusiastic about admitting another slave state to the Union. Only after great effort would the U.S. Congress be induced to even recognize Texas as a nation. Statehood would have to wait another decade.

Slavery was the central factor that would control the annexation discussion. But we must not frame the discussion of slavery into a solely political box. Slavery was a horror of the first order which would ultimately contribute to the cause of the United States Civil War, in which an equal number of Americans died than in all other wars in American history combined. Half of the Anglos who fought in that war did so on behalf of the Union, in part to correct this horrible blight and to establish Freedom for all. It is terrible to think that Freedom was once not universal. As we consider history, however, we do so with eyes forward as one people who together have a vested interest in a Freedom which is common to all. It should be noted that Mexico outlawed slavery per se, but effectively promoted it by allowing people to be placed in indentured servanthood for up to ninety-nine years. The effect was the same—it was slavery without the label. Even going back to Spanish claims on the land, we see Spain's early intentions in the New World were to enrich the motherland using cheap forced labor of the indigenous people, a practice they called *encomienda.*

Santa Anna is Released

One month after Sam Houston's inauguration as president of the Republic, he released Santa Anna from captivity on November 25 and sent him under escort to Washington D. C., where the vanquished dictator arrived on January 18, 1837. Santa Anna in his memoirs speaks of his journey:

> On taking leave of me, Houston said with emotion of pleasure, "General, you are no longer a prisoner. From this moment you are at absolute liberty. I want to ask one favor, and this I must surely merit: Before returning to your country, you visit President Jackson, my protector and friend. You will be well received by him because he wishes to know you." In that helpless state, and with good grace I offered to gladly comply with his wishes. I received a most cordial reception from President Jackson.

Santa Anna was pleased to have an escort to the United States and preferred this circuitous route home as a matter of personal safety.

Houston's purpose for Santa Anna's mission to Washington, D. C., was to have him indicate to the American president that Mexico would make no further attempt to conquer Texas, and have no objection to her independence.

The dictator met with President Jackson and William Wharton, who had been appointed Minister to the United States by Houston. Much was discussed, from official recognition, to annexation, to the purchase of Texas from Mexico as a way of allaying any future claims Mexico might make on Texas. The latter option was strongly opposed by Minister Wharton, who demanded Texas be party to any deal as an independent nation.

In the waning days of the Jackson administration—he would leave office on March 4—and against the political winds of the U.S. Congress and the president-elect, a rider was attached to an appropriation bill giving the president the authority to appoint a Minister to Texas once he had received satisfactory evidence that Texas was an independent power.

And so it came to pass on March 3, 1837, as the clock approached midnight on the last day of Jackson's administration, that the president acted on his newly acquired authority and named Alcee LaBranche of Louisiana to be Charge d'Affairs to the Republic of Texas. Though statehood would have to wait a decade, at least the nation of Texas was officially recognized. And on the stroke of midnight, the now former President Jackson, Minister Wharton, and a gathering of their friends drank to the Republic of Texas.

The Father of Texas

Stephen Austin had been elected Secretary of State in September 1836. It was then fifteen years since he had first ridden down into the Colorado-Brazos country to select a site for his first colony. He was only twenty-eight then and had given these years fully to his enterprise, to the neglect of his personal life and health. He had hoped to live in peace under the Mexican Government but ultimately faced the fact that the only path forward was independence. He was a reticent, silent man with great energy, and much of the work of constructing a new government now fell to him as Secretary of State. Texas was his life, labor, and love. He had no children and his people called him "Father." Indeed, he was the Father of Texas.

In the barn-like building that was the Old Columbia State House, he labored day and night executing the affairs of State by candlelight. As the winter set in, he would pull his cloak around his weak body and sit alone on his rawhide chair.

In a letter to a friend dated October 30, 1836, Austin lamented,

> . . . I have no house, not a roof in all Texas that I can call my own. The only one I had was burned at San Felipe during the late invasion of the enemy. I make my home where the business of the country calls me . . . I have no farm, no cotton plantation, no income, no money, no comforts. I have spent the prime of my life and worn out my constitution trying to colonize this country ... (for I am still in debt for the expenses of my trip to Mexico in 1833, '34, and '35) . . . Where my health and strength and time have gone . . . is in the service of Texas, and I am therefore not ashamed of my present poverty.

Only days later, he caught pneumonia. Death came quickly, the years of imprisonment and hardship having taken their toll on his slender frame. He passed away on December 27, at the age of forty-three. In his dying delirium, he relived his years in Texas, and his last words were, "The independence of Texas is recognized! Don't you see it in the papers?"

And this brings us to the close of his eventful life, and of the all-eventful year, 1836, in Texas history:

Independence was declared on March 2.

The Alamo had fallen on March 6.

Fannin fell at Goliad on March 27.

San Jacinto was won on April 21.

Houston was elected president on September 3.

The first Congress met on October 3.

And in the last days of the year, Stephen Fuller Austin passed away, having seen his life's work fulfilled. He was instrumental in moving fifteen hundred families comprised of eight thousand settlers into the Texas territory. He was the inspiration, backbone, security blanket, lobbyist, and heartbeat of the country and state-of-mind called "Texas."

The Capitals of Texas

It would seem natural that San Felipe de Austin would become the capital of Texas, but when Houston's militia retreated from there during the Runaway Scrape in April '36, the town was razed to keep anything of value from falling into enemy hands. Santa Anna had reached San Felipe while the fires were still smoldering and reported finding it in ruins.

The Texas Government was migratory during 1836. Following the March convention when independence had been declared at Washington-on-the-Brazos, the government retreated to Harrisburg and then to Galveston. President Burnet's headquarters was for a while at Velasco, and then Columbia where the first Congress met that October.

"Houston on Buffalo Bayou," as it was written in the Congressional Record of that day, was selected as the temporary capital on November 30, 1836, to serve in that capacity until 1840.

The city of Houston had just been surveyed three months prior, and only then had the Allen brothers, John and Augustus, begun advertising its development. Future governor Francis Lubbock tells of coming up Buffalo Bayou looking for the city aboard the steamboat *Laura* in January 1837 and passing it, finding no evidence of a landing or any improvements. He describes the "city" this way:

> Upon landing we found stakes and footprints. A few tents were located not far away, one large one was used for a saloon. Logs were being hauled from the forest for the erection of a hotel . . .

The Allen brothers began construction of a capitol building in April 1837 at the intersection of Main and Texas Streets, the current site of the Rice Hotel building in downtown Houston. The second session of the first Congress of the Republic of Texas convened on this site at noon on May 5, 1837. It was agreed that the permanent capital city would be named "Austin" in honor of the recently deceased Father of Texas. In the coming few years, various sites would be studied for its location.

In April 1838 it was voted that Austin would be located next to the town of La Grange, but President Houston vetoed the act, presumably because he wanted the capital to stay in Houston, his namesake settlement. Following the election of Mirabeau B. Lamar as Texas' second president, a commission was formed which selected the site of Waterloo on the east bank of the Colorado River in 1839. This location is the site of present-day Austin, Texas. At the time, Waterloo was the home of four frontier families and was far into Comanche country. Interestingly, Stephen Austin had chosen the same site years before as the location for his personal home where he had hoped to retire and live in peace, although this fact does not seem to have been known by the committee that chose it to bear his name.

Statehood or Independence?

Texas' time as a nation was anything but tranquil. It had amassed tremendous debt paying for the Revolution and was left with no credit at home or abroad. The Indians were up in arms as they rebelled against the extermination policies of Texas' second president, Mirabeau B. Lamar, in sharp contrast to the policies of Sam Houston. Lamar had also sought to expand the footprint of Texas into the New Mexico territory west of the claimed boundary of the Rio Grande River as it meandered to its source in the Rocky Mountains. His plan to boost the failing Texas economy manifested itself in the Santa Fe Expedition in 1841, the goal of which was to take control of the prosperous Santa Fe Trail. The expedition, however, had the exact opposite effect as the entire Texas force surrendered to Mexican authorities without a shot being fired, a victim of the harsh terrain more than anything else. Meanwhile Santa Anna, who was in and out of power, increased hostilities as he sought to retake what he had lost, sending various incursions back into Texas.

Santa Anna had unilaterally disavowed the secret Velasco Treaty due to his being incarcerated immediately following the treaty's execution. That was clearly a violation of the provision that called for his immediate release. While the government of the Republic was not responsible for his incarceration by the renegade militia, his abduction was, nonetheless, contrary to the government's responsibility to immediately deliver him to Mexico. The government was powerless to do anything about it at the time given that the regular militia was busy following the Mexican Army back across the Rio Grande. Nonetheless, the detainment did provide some justification for Santa Anna's failure to honor the treaty's terms.

Mexico presumably could have taken Texas back militarily without too much difficulty were it not for the constant internal political conflicts that occupied her time and resources all throughout this period. Mexico did, in fact, make repeated but anemic attempts to do so. The crutch that saved Texas during these isolated and trying times was the relentless stream of American immigrants coming into the Republic. The population, which at the time of the Revolution was thirty thousand, would grow to one hundred thousand in one decade.

Diplomatic Chess

The citizens of the new Republic had voted overwhelmingly in 1836 to enter the American Union if the United States would have them, but the American abolitionists brought great pressure to bear on the U.S. Congress and defeated an annexation bill in the House of Representatives so soundly that hope for its eventual success was largely abandoned. It would not be until 1845 that President John Tyler's crusade for Texas' statehood would succeed in the last few days of his presidency.

The question of statehood for Texas was the largest issue before the American people from 1843 to 1846 and drove the U.S. presidential election of 1844. This very issue kept Henry Clay out of the presidency and wrecked the Whig Party (the primary predecessor to today's Republican Party). It defeated the nomination of Martin Van Buren as the Democratic Party candidate in 1844 and was responsible for causing the election of the first "dark horse" candidate to the U.S. presidency—James K. Polk. It resulted in the keenest diplomatic game played on this continent for a century, in which the frontier folks of Texas won over the representatives of England and France. It stopped the aggressions of England in North America, played a powerful part in the acquisition of

Oregon, and resulted in a war between the United States and Mexico which would carry the American flag to the Pacific Ocean.

Following the congressional defeat of annexation in 1837, the issue of statehood remained dormant both in Texas and the U.S. for five years. These were dark and gloomy years for the young nation, which was broke, weak, and derided abroad. An 1837 financial crisis in the U.S. and subsequent years of depression left many in the southern United States bankrupt, and Texas became an asylum for fugitive debtors. Sheriffs in the United States who served writs to debtors would often simply write on them "G. T." or "G. T. T." when they were unable to locate their subjects. It meant "Gone to Texas."

During these troubled years, Mexico continued to be torn by its own revolutions and was never able to mount a large-scale expedition to re-conquer Texas, but it continued sending marauding forces across the Rio Grande to plunder and harass the people, twice going as far as San Antonio. During one such incursion in September 1842, San Antonio was captured and many of its citizens were abducted. Meanwhile the Indians were constantly being stirred up by Mexican agents, and their raids on the Texas settlers increased. The killings and theft amounted to a predatory warfare.

When Sam Houston entered his second presidency in 1842, he found the fortunes of Texas at a low ebb. Seeing little hope for annexation by the United States, he turned his attention to a European alliance, and with the highest diplomatic skill, he played a game with

England which became the chief factor in reversing the anti-Texas-statehood policy of the political powers in the American northeast. The wedge he would use to change their collective mind was the one thing the United States hated as much as slavery—England.

Ironically, France had thrown Louisiana, which included Texas, to Spain in 1762 to keep it out of England's hands. Napoleon had sold it under duress to the United States in 1803 to keep it from England. Now forty years later after many changes in sovereignty, the fear of England gaining a foothold in Texas would drive the United States to annex Texas and to wage war with Mexico.

In 1842 John Tyler was president of the United States, a Democrat out of step with his own party, who staked his political fortunes on annexing Texas. He sent word to President Houston that he would like to open negotiations for an annexation treaty. But the old Cherokee chief feigned not to hear his overtures and continued his open parleys with England. Houston's plan was to court England, who had influence over Mexico, and have the British use their influence to fix a truce between Mexico and Texas such that Mexico would stop the eternal guerrilla warfare on the border and acknowledge Texas independence. If he could convince the United States that he was serious about this alliance with England, he just might be able to sway the U.S. to annex Texas in order to block England from increasing its influence in the New World via Texas. The Republic of Texas even opened an embassy in London, and the site can still be visited today.

Mexico was anxious to stop the annexation of Texas by the U.S. and had its eyes on one day reclaiming Texas militarily. Houston, though he was a proponent of U.S. annexation, could not appear to favor the idea for fear of alienating English aid. And if President Tyler should fail in his annexation efforts, Texas could be left feeble at home and friendless abroad. Houston was playing a complicated game of diplomatic chess masterfully.

Eventually the Tyler administration would provide assurances of aid to Texas against any Mexican threats should annexation negotiations fail, and Houston finally consented. In December 1843 the Texas Congress voted to authorize a treaty of annexation to the U.S. The proceedings had been closely guarded to prevent any information about it from leaking to the United States. In fact, the treaty was signed before virtually any American citizens became aware of it.

Now the treaty had to go before the U.S. Congress for ratification. The American public was shocked to learn of its existence and that realization provoked wild protests in the North and East. Rumors circulated in the United States that the proposed British-Texas treaty would allow Texas to market all of its exports to the British Empire and Texas would also have access to duty-free manufactured goods. The concept included prohibiting all American manufactured articles from the Texas market.

That and the problem of slavery caused fiery anti-slavery activist and Boston-based publisher William Garrison to exclaim, "Those who would befriend Texas would dethrone God." John Quincy Adams saw the doom of humanity in the proposed treaty, speaking of it in terms of causing the dissolution of the American Union. A Boston newspaper wrote, "We have territory enough, bad morals enough, public debt enough, slavery enough, without adding Texas."

It seemed to be a foregone conclusion that the treaty would not pass the U.S. Senate, but the stage was set for the U.S. presidential election of 1844. James K. Polk would be elected president after the incumbent, John Tyler, withdrew from the race and threw his support to him. Polk, like Tyler, was a strong supporter of annexation, but many in Texas feared the United States would never accept Texas given the many times it had been denied. And the London *Times* declared that the election of Polk "was the triumph of all that was worst in American life," while the London *Morning Post* wrote of Polk, "The Republican monster must be checked" for his desire to annex Texas.

Meanwhile Mexico, angered at the turn of events, gave notice that hostilities were renewed, and Santa Anna, who was once again in power, began to at least feign preparations to wage a campaign against Texas by land and sea. President Tyler just might have to make good on his promise to aid Texas and safeguard her independence. As a subject of international politics, the Republic of Texas occupied no small place in the diplomacy of three of the world's principle powers—the United States, England, and France—not to mention Mexico.

Houston's game of diplomatic chess was having its intended effect in the United States. A resolution for annexation passed both the U.S. House and Senate. President Tyler signed it February 27, 1845, just five days before his term of office expired, but there was still much work to do before it could be enacted, not the least of which was that Texas now had to agree to the changes the U.S. Congress had made to it. The agreement gave Texas until January 1, 1846, to accept the counteroffer.

Anson Jones

Meanwhile, back in Texas Anson Jones had been elected as the fourth president of Texas a few months earlier and continued down the road with England and France regarding an independent Texas and recognition by Mexico. Jones believed that if Mexico could be brought to recognize Texas independence, then he favored independence, as opposed to American statehood. The message that the United States Congress and its president had acted on annexation had not yet reached him. Jones was conferring with his government and representatives of England and France, and on March 29 they agreed in principal that Texas would stay an independent nation so long as Mexico acknowledged the fact. Envoys were sent to Mexico to finalize negotiations. So, when Colonel Andrew Jackson Donelson, United States Representative to the Republic of Texas and nephew of former American President Andrew Jackson, arrived with the United States' offer on April 1, he was not received well. Even Sam Houston, who was living at his home in Huntsville at the time, viewed the U.S. offer unfavorably, citing sharp objections to the changes made by the U.S. Congress.

President Jones meanwhile was receiving strong pressure to convene Congress from the largely pro-annexation Texas citizens while all kinds of rumors were afloat regarding his opposition to annexation. The rumors were so loud that the Mexican Consul at New Orleans advised his government that a revolution in Texas was imminent. Santa Anna, for his part, was out of power again and in exile, but he would return the next year. And England and France were pressing Mexico hard to accept an independent Texas with the argument to Mexico that, "The acquisition of Texas by the United States made that detested country [the U.S.] the next-door neighbor of Mexico, and an effort [by the U.S.] would follow to conquer and annex Mexico."

It was a race against the clock. The negotiators in Mexico knew that the only hope they had to defeat annexation lay in returning to Texas quickly with a treaty between the two countries in hand. President Jones had succumbed to the pressure of the people and called upon Congress to meet in June for the purpose of taking up the issue of annexation. And numerous reports reached Mexico that the United States was sending warships into the Gulf of Mexico and massing troops on the Texas frontier.

Finally in May 1845, the delegation to Mexico returned to Texas armed with an agreement to make a treaty acknowledging Texas independence on condition it would not unite with the United States.

Dr. Anson Jones, president of Texas, was a good man but not an artist in the game of political duplicity and diplomacy. He was trying to play Sam Houston without the ability or experience. Eventually he would be driven out of public life for his willingness to form an alliance with England against the United States. As for now, he excitedly made a public announcement of the Mexican treaty, essentially offering his people the choice to remain independent with guarantees of territorial integrity or to become part of the American Union. But the news, instead of being received in this spirit, roused a storm all over Texas which may have overthrown his government except for the fact that he had called for Congress to convene in less than thirty days to take up this issue.

The Last Act of the Great Drama of Annexation

The Ninth Congress of the Republic of Texas met in extraordinary session at Washington-on-the-Brazos on June 16, 1845. The sentiment of the people of Texas is shown by the fact that annexation was accepted by the unanimous vote of both houses of Congress, and the Mexican treaty was unanimously rejected. A convention was then called to meet on July 4 to form a state constitution and set up a state government. In the interim, news came of the death of former U.S. President Andrew Jackson, who had played a powerful role in the history of Texas. Jackson was of Scottish ancestry and harbored a deep-seated hatred for England. He had never forgotten that, as a boy during the American Revolution, a British officer cruelly hit him for refusing to shine the officer's boots. He carried that scar into international history.

In the July convention, annexation was ratified with only one vote against it. This convention formulated Texas' State Constitution of 1845, which was ratified by the people of Texas in November. The Constitution was then presented through President Polk to the American Congress, and on December 29, 1845, Texas was formally admitted to the Union as the twenty-eighth state.

News of the annexation was received with great delight and relief by the citizens of Texas. The celebration of Texas is illustrated in a scene described by Noah Smithwick, who as a nineteen-year-old boy had come alone to Texas in 1827. Since that time Smithwick had blacksmithed Bowie knives under contract with James Bowie himself in San Felipe de Austin; had been declared a "bad citizen" and deported to Louisiana for helping a friend escape prison; had returned to Texas to join the Revolution, fighting in the Battle of Concepción; had negotiated treaties with the Indians as an Indian agent; and had served as a Texas Ranger in the Bastrop area from 1836–38. Smithwick was in attendance in Judge Robert Baylor's District Court when the good tidings came by messenger:

> District court was in session in Bastrop when the news came that the bill for the annexation of Texas had passed the United States Congress and received the approval of President Polk. Judge Robert E. B. Baylor

[who was by all accounts a fine man of faith and intellect; he was a lawyer, judge, and ordained minister; he did not drink, cuss, or use words carelessly; and later founded Baylor University], who was presiding, in announcing the glad tidings . . . said that "No man [would] be considered drunk . . . so long as he could pronounce the word 'Epsom'" . . . and he therefore adjourned court till 10 o'clock the next morning, that we might celebrate, and celebrate we did with a will.

In the absence of cannon, we brought out all the anvils the town could muster and taking up a collection to pay for [gun] powder, proceeded to get all the noise possible out of them. Had there been any Indians anywhere in hearing they would probably have gotten away from that vicinity in short order ... Judge Baylor, Baptist preacher though he was, made a full hand with the boys [in other words, he uncustomarily took a strong drink with them in celebration!].

My recollection of the details is not quite clear; therefore, I will not undertake to say whether we stopped at "Epsom" or not, but we were all on hand at ten next morning.

Texas celebrated. But Mexico, which had repeatedly declared that it would consider the annexation of Texas by the United States to be an act of war, was massing its whole force on the Texas border for an invasion. Mexico would, in fact, face off against the United States Army in a few months in what would become known as the

Mexican War. This war would last two years and settle once and for all the question of Texas sovereignty and borders. A direct result of the war would be the acquisition by the United States of all the territory west of Texas to the Pacific Ocean.

On February 16, 1846, the first Legislature of the State of Texas met in Austin. Republic of Texas President Anson Jones formally closed the affairs of the Republic and surrendered his office to the governor.

The span of life of the Republic of Texas was two weeks shy of ten years.

Three days later, on February 19, Smithwick describes:

> ... the most touching scene in the brief drama of the Republic, when Anson Jones, its last President, standing on the steps of the old capitol, lowered the old flag from the mast [see Figure 10] and reverently furling it, announced amidst breathless silence, "The Republic of Texas is no more." Many a head was bowed, many a broad chest heaved, and many a manly cheek was wet with tears when that broad field of blue in the center of which, like a signal light, glowed the lone star, emblem of the sovereignty of Texas, was furled and laid away among the relics of the dead Republic.

The Republic of Texas was no more, but the fruits of the men and women who sacrificed their livelihoods and their lives to tame this wilderness and to banish oppression in the name of Freedom, live on.

EPILOGUE

Today we enjoy the same freedoms won by our Texas forefathers but under the flag of the United States. The first settlers who moved into this territory understood the price of Freedom and were willing to risk and sacrifice so much for it. The love of Freedom was a shared value among the settlers who earned the title of Patriot simply because they gave themselves to Freedom's Higher Good.

Twenty-six-year-old lawyer William Barret Travis and 188 other combatants inside the Alamo knowingly went to their graves not in pursuit of their own pleasure, but for a cause they considered greater than themselves.

The reluctant warrior and former governor of Tennessee Sam Houston risked everything against all odds because he esteemed Freedom so highly.

Entrepreneur Stephen F. Austin spent his health in pursuit of this ideal on behalf of others.

And forty-seven-year-old Lorenzo de Zavala fled his country in the face of rising tyranny to become a hunted man because he would not subject himself to tyranny's reign.

Every man and woman in the story who stood for the Higher Good, both the named and unnamed, both the known and unknown, engaged in the process to win this luxury we call Freedom.

As long as free people exist, those people will continue to write the epilogue to this story. We are writing it today. Together we can write another chapter—or allow someone else to write "The End." Let us always remember Crockett's "almighty idea of universal independence"—in a word, Freedom—from his March 2 Alamo journal. We are today, in Crockett's words, "the children of those who have freely shed their blood" for Freedom. Let us never trample upon this great gift they gave to you and to me. Let us engage in the work of Freedom's preservation.

The price of Liberty is eternal vigilance.

AFTERTHOUGHTS ON FREEDOM

The heroes of the Republic's freedom fight shout to us in the present to engage in the process of preserving the institution of Freedom for ourselves and for our children. Once Freedom is established by the sacrifices of others, it becomes a legacy to be passed on by wise fiscal, political, and societal engagement. Only by continuing in this responsibility can any people ensure it as their legacy to the next generation.

In the politics of free nations, threats to the institution of Freedom can come from both the extreme political Right and the extreme political Left. These threats can appear as an internal political power consolidation into an individual or group, taking the form of a frontal assault that is often easy to identify. They can also present themselves as soft-sold socialism with a benevolent face pasted on it—a gradual backdoor invasion in which the victim invites the invader in naively. They can rise from non-political sources that attempt to undermine the fabric of free society. And they can come externally by way of military assault. Regardless, the result is always the same—consolidated power, tyranny, oppression, and poverty. Freedom and civil rights are lost.

In the United States we have a three-pronged system of checks and balances that prevent an internal power consolidation quite effectively. Attempts are afoot, however, to weaken this balance of power through broadening the authority of the Executive Branch and/or through weakening the authority of the Judicial Branch.

One needs to look no further than Venezuela, which not long ago subordinated their Judiciary to their Executive Branch in a gradual process of institutional weakening and political power consolidation. This slight adjustment to checks and balances was done intentionally to concentrate power and has ultimately caused the rule of law to become virtually nonexistent in that nation. The predictable result has been tyranny, oppression, and the destruction of free society.

And one does not have to look far to see the assaults on the fabric of our society—the "demonizing of all things America"—while disregarding the extraordinarily positive impact America has had on the uplifting of humanity both internally and across the globe.

America, even with all its faults, is the flag bearer for both Freedom and stability in the world. America is the only nation with enough strength and remnant of moral fiber that is capable of keeping order in a world tending towards chaos. Free societies can only exist on the foundation of order, and the very existence of other free nations depends directly on the ability of the United States to lead in maintaining stability in the world. If left to the anti-freedom powers, chaos would prevail, and the governing force of chaos is tyranny.

Do not be deceived by the vain hope that enemies to free societies are willing to just let the United States exist in a live-and-let-live world. Some people and some nations hate the freedoms found here and wish to subjugate us just as they have subjugated their own people. They hate informed free people because those people will not subject themselves to tyrants' control, or in some cases, pledge allegiance to their fanaticism masquerading as religion. America is a target because its strength allows other freedom-minded people to institutionalize Freedom and civil rights in their own domains under the umbrella of the worldwide American security apparatus. If this worldwide American security umbrella fails, so do all free governments across the globe.

Let us be thankful that, in the case of slavery, this abomination has been righted in America such that Freedom is now for all. And let us know that Freedom is not a gift given once that lasts forever. Rather it is a gift that must be actively preserved, lest it be destroyed by those who cannot tolerate free people, because free people refuse to be controlled by the very tyrants that seek to destroy them. Freedom is never perpetuated by weakness—this is true in government, in the military, in society, in the financial world, and in personal lives. Freedom requires individuals and groups to hold the ideal to be greater than themselves and to make sometimes hard decisions in life and government that will sustain it. We must come to understand once again that unless individuals and factions hold themselves to be less important than the institution of Freedom and the Common Good, Freedom will be lost in the here and now.

Let us unite around political common ground that puts preserving the institution of Freedom first. Let us unite around this ideal that always uplifts humanity in a dark world. Let us unite around the need to move our societal focus from the "deck chairs on the *Titanic*" to the leaks that can sink the ship. Let us educate those who are unknowledgeable of the ongoing price of Freedom that each of us must pay forward. Let us each consider the Common Good before we make choices for self. Let us look to the Republic for inspiration to face the enemies of Freedom both from within and from without.

E Pluribus Unum —"Out of Many, One"

SOURCES AND ACKNOWLEDGMENTS

MUCH OF THE NARRATIVE AND MANY OF THE FACTS IN this book have been compiled from early authors who wrote their history either from personal experience or while the history was fresh on peoples' minds. My source materials largely exist in the public domain, their copyrights having expired, and I quote liberally from those works. Where I have done so, I do not claim their words as my own. Credit is given to these well-respected historians for recording the history for future generations. Special acknowledgment to Clarence Wharton, author of *The Republic of Texas*, whose writing style and handling of the historical narrative was a great source of content and inspiration. In my desire to deliver a summary overview of the history of the Republic of Texas, his work proved to be extremely helpful.

SOURCES

Bancroft, Hubert H. *The Works of Hubert Howe Bancroft*. Volume 16, *North American States and Texas, Volume II 1801–1889*. San Francisco: The History Company Publishers, 1889.

Barker, Eugene C. *The Life of Stephen F. Austin, Founder of Texas, 1793–1836: A Chapter in the Westward Movement of the Anglo-American People*. Nashville: Cokesbury Press, 1926.

———. "The San Jacinto Campaign." *The Quarterly of the Texas State Historical Association* 4, no. 4, 1901: 237–345. This includes the primary documents "Houston's Report of the Battle" (1836); "Extract from Santa Anna's Report" (1837); "Extracts from Moseley Baker's Letter to Houston" (1844); "Delgado's Account of the Battle" (1849); "Kuykendall's Recollections of the Campaign" (1856); "Labadie's Account of the Campaign" (1859); "R. J. Calder's Recollections of the Campaign" (1861); and "Amasa Turner's Account of the Battle" (1874).

Crockett, David. *Col. Crockett's exploits and adventures in Texas: wherein is contained a full account of his journey from Tennessee to the Red River and Natchitoches, and thence across Texas to San Antonio, including his many hair-breadth escapes: together with a topographical, historical and political view of Texas*. Philadelphia: T. K. and P. G. Collins, 1836. [This book was published posthumously by a journalist and lawyer named Richard Penn Smith, who added a final chapter, detailing events after Crockett's last journal entry.]

Foote, Henry Stuart. *Texas and the Texans: Advance of the Anglo-Americans to the South-West*. Philadelphia: Thomas, Cowperthwait & Company, 1841.

Holley, Mary Austin. *Texas*. Baltimore: Armstrong & Plaskitt, 1833.

Hunt, David Glenn. "*Vito Alessio Robles: Coahuila y Texas, Desde la Consumacion de la Independencia*

Hasta el Traitado de Paz de Guadalupe Hidalgo, (Mexico, 1946): An Edited Translation of Volume II, Chapters 1–7." Masters thesis, Southern Methodist University, 1950.

Johnson, Frank, and Eugene Barker. *A History of Texas and Texans*. Chicago: American Historical Society, 1914.

Lynn, John J. *Reminiscences of Fifty Years in Texas*. New York: D. & J. Sadlier & Company, 1883.

Newell, Chester. *History of the Revolution in Texas, Particularly of the War of 1835 & '36*. New York: Wiley & Putnam, 1838.

Parker, A. A. *Trip to the West and Texas Comprising a Journey of Eight Thousand Miles, through New York, Michigan, Illinois, Missouri, Louisiana and Texas, in the Autumn and Winter of 1834–5*. Concord, New Hampshire: William White, and Boston: Benjamin B. Mussey, 1836.

Rives, George Lockhart. *The United States and Mexico 1821–1848*. New York: Charles Scribner's Sons, 1913.

Santa Anna, Antonio López de, D. Ramón Martinez Caro, Vicente Filísola, José Urrea, and José María Tornel y Mendívil. Translated by Carlos E. Casteñeda. *The Mexican Side of the Texan Revolution*. Dallas: P. L. Turner, 1928. [Primarily used were Santa Anna's *Manifesto Relative to His Operations in the Texas Campaign and His Capture* (1837), and José Urrea's *Diary of the Military Operations of the Division Which Under His Command Campaigned in Texas* (1838).]

Smithwick, Noah. *The Evolution of a State, or Recollections of Old Texas Days*. Austin: Gammel Book Company, 1900.

Wharton, Clarence R. *The Republic of Texas*. Houston: C. C. Young Printing Company, 1922.

Winters, James Washington. "An Account of the Battle of San Jacinto." *The Quarterly of the Texas State Historical Association* 6, no. 2, 1902: 139–44.

Wooten, Dudley G. *A Comprehensive History of Texas 1685–1897, Volume 1*. Dallas: William G. Scarff, 1898.

Yoakum, Henderson K. *History of Texas from its First Settlement in 1685 to its Annexation to the United States in 1846*. New York: Redfield, 1855.

SUGGESTED FURTHER READING

Texas' history is so rich, it is no wonder that there are literally thousands of books written about it, going all the way back to its earliest days. Here are a few books that I personally recommend.

Col. Crockett's Exploits and Adventures in Texas, by David Crockett. This book, originally published in 1836, is truly an adventure worth experiencing. You will find Crockett's humor, insight, and wisdom, and you will live his journey to Texas. Available in reprint.

The Evolution of a State, or Recollections of Old Texas Days, by Noah Smithwick. By reputation this is one of the best firsthand accounts of early Texas life from a man who lived here from 1827 until the advent of the Civil War. Smithwick, blind and in his nineties, dictated his memoirs to his daughter prior to his death in 1899. His daughter published the book in 1900. Available in reprint.

From the Plains to the Pulpit, by John Wesley Anderson. Another firsthand account, this one describes the prairie lands west of Houston in the last half of the nineteenth century (the book was published in 1907). Anderson lived and worked in the area of Addicks, Waller, Hockley, Hempstead, and Cane Island (Katy,

Texas) as a cowboy and later a preacher. Great local Houston color. His descriptions of wildlife on the Katy prairie are astounding. He would travel as far west as the Cavender Ranch on the Frio River near Leakey, Texas. Available in reprint.

Lone Star: A History of Texas and the Texans. This bestseller by T. R. Fehrenbach provides a detailed and scholarly study of Texas from before Christ to the twentieth century by one of Texas' most respected historians. Still in print.

The Texas Rangers: A Century of Frontier Defense, by Walter Prescott Webb, one of the most respected historians of Texas and the West. This 1935 book tells the story of the greatest body of man hunters ever assembled in America. It truly reads better than fiction. Still in print.

The Texas State Historical Association is the oldest learned society in our state, dating back to 1897. Its mission is to foster the appreciation, understanding, and teaching of the rich and unique history of Texas. Wonderful resources are available through this organization and many can be found at www.tshaonline.org

Wise About Texas Podcasts, by Judge Ken Wise. *Wise About Texas* presents Texas history in an engaging, scholarly, and interesting way. You will learn more about the Texas history you know and a lot about Texas history you don't know. Available on Apple Podcasts and all other podcast platforms.

Illustration Credits

FIGURE 1. Public Domain
FIGURE 2. Copyright © 2024 Blake Pfeffer. Drawings by Anne McLaughlin, Blue Lake Design
FIGURE 3. Copyright © 2024 Blake Pfeffer. Drawings by Anne McLaughlin, Blue Lake Design
FIGURE 4. Copyright © 2024 Blake Pfeffer. Drawings by Anne McLaughlin, Blue Lake Design
FIGURE 5. 1/103-722, Courtesy of Texas State Library and Archives Commission
FIGURE 6. Courtesy of DeGolyer Library, SMU. Lawrence T. Jones, III Texas Photographs Collection
FIGURE 7. Drawings by Anne McLaughlin, Blue Lake Design. Used with permission
FIGURE 8. Drawings by Anne McLaughlin, Blue Lake Design. Used with permission
FIGURE 9. Drawings by Anne McLaughlin, Blue Lake Design. Used with permission
FIGURE 10. Drawings by Anne McLaughlin, Blue Lake Design. Used with permission
COVER PHOTO The door to the Sacristy of the Alamo Chapel. This is the actual door that the Alamo defenders would have used during the siege of 1836. Susanna Dickinson and her eighteen-month-old baby hid behind this door during the siege. Courtesy of Edd and Nina Hendee and Taste of Texas Restaurant. The door is currently on display at the Taste of Texas Restaurant in Houston, Texas.

About the Author

Blake Pfeffer lives in Houston, Texas, and has been enamored with Texas history since he was a young teenager. He has been in the mortgage business since 1990, in addition to managing and developing the family farm in Waller County along with his brother Kirk. He received his undergraduate degree from the University of Texas in Finance and also Engineering Route to Business. He is the father of four adult children and husband of thirty-four years to his favorite Texan, Jeanne.

Colophon

Book edited and designed by Kit Sublett for Whitecaps Media

Cover jacket designed by Anne McLaughlin for Blue Lake Design

Main body composed in Fanwood Text at 11/13.5, designed by Barry Schwartz as a revival of the classic Fairfield font

www.texashistorybook.com